Once Upon a Time at La Napoule

THE MEMOIRS OF MARIE CLEWS

Once Upon a Time at La Napoule

THE MEMOIRS OF MARIE CLEWS

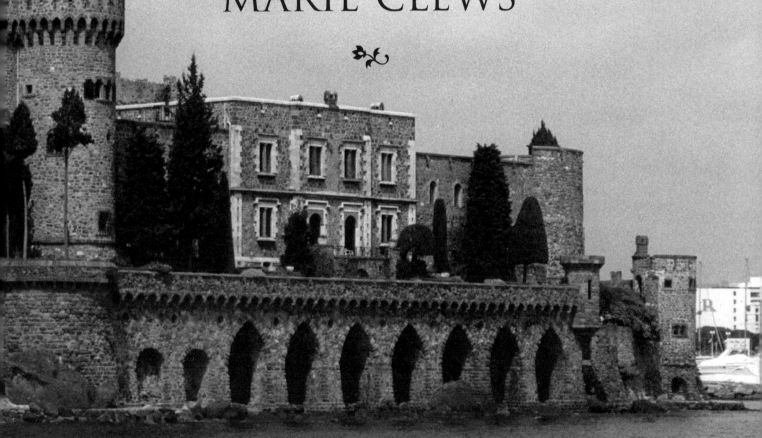

Introduction by Mancha Madison Clews
Afterword by Margaret Strawbridge Clews

Library of Congress Cataloging-in-Publication Data

Clews, Marie, 1880–1959.
    Once upon a time at La Napoule : the memoirs of Marie Clews / introduction by Mancha Madison Clews ; afterword by Margaret Strawbridge Clews. — 2nd ed.
        p.   cm.
        ISBN 1-889833-0307 (alk. paper)
        1. Clews, Marie, 1880–1959. 2. Sculptors' spouses—United States—Biography.
3. La Napoule Art Foundation, Henry Clews Memorial. 4. Clews, Henry, 1876–1937—
Art patronage. I Title.
        NB237.C55A2 1998
        730 ' .92--dc21
        [B]

                                                                                98-5230
                                                                                CIP

Published by Memoirs Unlimited, Inc.
21 Lothrop Street, Beverly, Massachusetts 01915.

To order additional copies please contact:
La Napoule Art Foundation
799 South Street, Portsmouth NH 03801
e-mail LNAF@clews.org

Designed by Joyce C. Weston.
Printed in the United States of America.
Second edition.

Contents

At La Napoule: Mancha and Margaret Clews with Henry Clews's "The God of Humormystics"

Introduction
MANCHA MADISON CLEWS

❦

*T*O INTRODUCE THE MEMOIRS OF MARIE CLEWS, I thought I would add my own reminiscences and thoughts about growing up at La Napoule and about the gifted and remarkable people who created it—my mother and father.

I was a small child when my parents purchased La Napoule. In fact, their discovery of this beautiful site had in part to do with me. In the final year of World War I, we were living in Paris, but they decided to take me to the south of France for some months because of my poor health. I had contracted the Spanish flu—very dangerous for a toddler—and I was further weakened by having been fed some poor milk (mixed with water and thickened with chalk, they found out later). Good milk, along with other supplies, had been hard to come by in wartime Paris. On this trip my parents rented La Napoule for our holiday and fell in love with it. They bought the property, and we moved there permanently in 1919.

In those days, among the well off, children were brought up mostly by the servants, and this was the case for me. I was ushered in to see my parents usually once a day, decked out in perfectly neat clothes with everything tucked in nicely. On one such occasion, at about age five or so, I was presented after lunch while my parents were entertaining guests. As was the custom, after being introduced, I kissed all the ladies' hands; then I proceeded to kiss the tail of my brother Ogden's Great Dane and left the room amid much laughter, having no idea why they were amused!

I didn't see my parents much on a day-to-day basis, and my conversations with them were few. Because I grew up among the French servants, my first language was French. This made communicating with my parents awkward, since they spoke English together. (My father never became entirely fluent in French, though my mother eventually did; when I was older, she would often ask me to check her letters for correct French grammar and spelling.) Mother would tuck me in every night, perhaps tickle me a little and chat for a few moments, but that was about it.

To be perfectly honest, it was a lonely childhood. I didn't have any close friends. For a playmate I had Blanchette, the gardener's daughter, who was a few years older than me. Because I was often sick, I spent a lot of time with nurses and governesses. I would amuse myself by riding my bike or sailing my boat, usually by myself.

Before I went to boarding school, I learned English from Miss Coles. For many years she was indispensable to the smooth running of La Napoule. She acted as secretary to my father, helped supervise the servants, and generally managed the household. In an often lonely childhood, Miss Coles provided me with companionship and attention, taking me for walks, joining me on boat rides, and sharing picnics with me. An Englishwoman with the formidable first name of Ethelberte, she would fascinate me with her stories of working for members of the Russian aristocracy and her timely escape from Russia in the dangerous days of the revolution. She told me of a wolf-dog that had saved her life by holding her sleeve and leading her past soldiers who were killing the family she worked for.

On Sundays she took me with her to the Catholic church next to La Napoule. The priest had a strong Marseilles accent, and when, during the mass, he would refer to Saint Joseph as the Virgin Mary's "chaste époux" (chaste spouse), to me it sounded like "chasser les poux" (chase the lice). I wondered what lice had to do with religion!

At the age of eight, I began attending boarding school. Later I also had tutors, usually from Cambridge or Oxford, who helped me with my studies, the *devoirs de vacances,* during the summers. The tutor would stay in one of the towers. One time I rigged up a string from my room to the tower so that he could call me early in the morning for an outing we had planned. Once pulled, the string was supposed to start an electric motor near my bed, to wake me up. Unfortunately, the electric plug was faulty and it set my mosquito net on fire at two in the morning. My parents rushed in as my mattress caught fire, and we threw the mattress out the window. Thus my scientific curiosity almost destroyed the château!

Miss Coles with Mancha, 1923, and as he remembers her, 1934

While I was growing up, La Napoule was a work in progress. A new gatehouse was built, gardens were landscaped, a terrace supported by a dramatic arched wall was added to the waterfront, and the roof and chimneys were removed from the main house and replaced by a terrace and crenellated battlements. At the time of my older half sister Louise's wedding, the stairway was unusable, and she had to climb down a ladder in her wedding dress. The courtyard was often filled with activity. In fact, a narrow-gauge railway was set up on our property for a time, to help in transporting the stone from place to place. From my room I could see the Italian stonecutters chipping away with hammer and chisel on the stone. I amused myself by borrowing some tools from them and building a series of little roadways in stone. This small-scale highway planning interested me more than making sculpture.

My father was a most unusual character. He had withdrawn from society in order to dedicate his life to the creation of art and to shape a lifestyle reflecting the glories of the past. Yet despite his dedication to it, my father never tried to impart the artist's way of life to me. One time, when I was sick in bed, he did give me a bit of Plasticine, a green model-ing clay that he used. I made a little fish out of it, and he complimented me on how good it was. He liked the way I had used curves in shaping it. But this is almost my only recollection of sharing the experience of art with him.

My father called himself Mancha and considered himself a modern-day Don Quixote, a brave idealist and believer in romance in the midst of a corrupt, mean-spirited society. He called me Little Mancha. But though I was his namesake, we didn't really have heart-to-heart talks as father and son. On one occasion, when I was about sixteen, he expound-ed to me the philosophy of Nietszche, but he didn't encourage me to share my own ideas. I don't think he knew how to build rapport with a child or adolescent. He tended to say silly, flippant things to pass the time. Once, as we were riding in a car to the dentist, he made up silly names for me and asked how I'd like to be called by them.

Though many people have noted what a brilliant conversationalist he was, we never shared an easy conversational intimacy. Even when I was old enough to sit at table with my parents and their guests, it was expected that I would say nothing. My father generally dominated the talk, and the only person who could silence him was his own mother, who occasionally visited from New York. I can recall how, after one of my father's particularly long tirades, she looked at him and said firmly, "We've heard quite enough from you, Henry." Some of our visitors enjoyed taking him on in conversational duels, and he really seemed to enjoy these sallies. I think he was happiest in the company of well-read intellectuals with a yen for argument.

My father often held forth on his philosophy of life, which was def-initely opposed to the trends and values of his contemporary society. He was passionately committed to his ideals. Though some of them seem dated now, he did have an amusing, sardonic way of expressing them. Despite the fact that his sister was a leading voice in the U.S. feminist and suffragist movement, my father had opposing views, which he expressed in his only published work, *Mumbo-Jumbo* (1923) As he wrote:

> For those who prefer forests to newspapers, it must be extremely dis-tressing to see their beloved trees rapidly disappearing into machine pulp to be transmuted into untold million of tons of chronicled lies, gossip, scandal, criminality, pole-cat politics, charlatanism… (p. 34).

He also used strong terms to express his views on politics and social class:

> It is as unnatural and uninstinctive to have a mob-elected president as it would be for a hive to have a president bee.... I can think of nothing more satanically monotonous... than a world without class distinctions and populated with communal processional human caterpillars (p. 36).

I think he would have liked to have lived in an earlier era, perhaps back in the days of the court of Louis XIV, and he much preferred government by monarchy and aristocracy to that of democracy:

> Democrats and socialists are beauty-proof, and communists and syndicalists are humanity-proof (p. 14).

Though he himself was the son of a wealthy banker who had built his own fortune, my father considered himself a sort of aristocrat of the spirit, despite his lack of blue-blooded ancestry.

Here are a few of his thoughts concerning the machine age:

> I propose that we immediately begin to unmechanize, uninvent our way out of these scientific catacombs of unbelief, artificial pleasure, false happiness, machine idolatry, and suffocating vulgarity into the sunlight of belief, full-hearted Elizabethan merriment, self-expression, vital refinement, and true happiness.... The recent war [World War I] gave some idea to what extent man has become degenerated by science and machinery.... America...is the most mechanized, unspiritual country in the world, and consequently the most dangerous to true civilization. (pp. 61–64)

Despite his dislike of machines, La Napoule was equipped with electricity, central heating, modern plumbing, and telephones—though my father himself never used telephones. As fate would have it, from an early age I took a strong interest in electronics! As a teenager I built a radio with parts bought from local suppliers, yet, though he showed no interest in it himself, he made no fuss about my participation in the nasty world of machines. I kept my radio equipment in the gatehouse, with an antenna attached to one of the towers. My father didn't attempt to stunt my interest in electronics, even when—horror of horrors!—I decided to

Marie Clews with Ogden Goelet, her son by her first marriage to Robert Goelet.

take engineering studies at Cambridge. Overall, my mother seemed to take more of an interest in my education—and I always did very well at school.

Although a fierce social critic, my father was not particularly a reformer of society. Instead, he chose to retreat from it and try to live differently himself. Many people came to visit La Napoule to see my parents and their way of life. As might be expected, they did entertain many friends from the titled families of Europe. My mother's photo album contains many pictures of French, British, Russian, and Austrian countesses, dukes, and lords. Distinguished guests included the composer Frederick Delius, the conductor Sir Thomas Beecham, and Emerald Cunard, whom I found especially lively and entertaining. Winston Churchill visited while I was away at school in the mid-1930s, and Miss Coles later told me that Churchill believed that another European war and the resultant loss of life were simply inevitable to save England.

ONE POIGNANT ASPECT of my parents' married life at La Napoule is that it represented a starting over, a second chance for both of them. They had both lived through divorces, and each had two children from their former marriages.

In her memoirs my mother tells a good deal about my father's first marriage, but mentions little about hers. She had been married to the man considered the "catch" of his day—Robert Goelet of New York, whose wealth, according to newspaper accounts of the time, provided him with a daily income of $5,000 in 1904, the year of his marriage to my mother. She had been considered the most beautiful debutante in Philadelphia, and both families seemed delighted with the match. Society columns overflowed with lavish descriptions of the wedding, including the emerald-and-diamond necklace my mother wore, a gift from her new in-laws.

However, the union was marked by a great deal of discord—in part, it seems, because of my mother's love of the arts. She wished to surround herself with musicians and painters, and she herself enjoyed singing and painting; these activities were frowned upon by her new family and husband. Robert Goelet disliked the people his wife was bringing into their social circle.

She sought a divorce early in 1914, and again newspaper columnists eagerly reported the proceedings. My mother brought forth a number of witnesses who testified to Mr. Goelet's cruel behavior to her as the relationship foundered: he set his valet to spy on all her comings and goings, he eavesdropped on her telephone conversations, she was not allowed to entertain anyone in her home of whom her husband did not approve, and—despite his immense fortune—little food was kept on hand in the house, so if her own friends did visit, she could not offer them anything to eat. This controlling behavior, in effect keeping her in a gilded prison, was compounded by more abusive treatment. The judge granted her the divorce on grounds of "extreme cruelty and other gross misbehavior and wickedness."

Previous to the divorce, she had begun studying art with Henry Clews Jr. at his studio in Newport, Rhode Island. One can just imagine their sympathy for each other as they spoke of their artistic aspirations, how these had been stunted by their first marriages, and how they hoped to reclaim their dreams of devoting themselves to their true calling. In December 1914 they married. Though there were difficulties ahead—my mother was heart-broken to leave her two sons in the United States when she and my father moved to Paris, and he as well had two children (one in the custody of his first wife, and the other in his own parents' custody)—they struck off on a new, bold life together.

MY MOTHER HAD STUDIED PAINTING and loved opera. Though singing gave her great delight, it was generally acknowledged that, though sensitive in expression, her voice lacked real power. By marrying my father, she devoted herself to art by devoting herself to an artist.

It should not be underestimated how much she did to support my father's career, especially in the way she made up for his weaknesses. Where he tended to be delicate in health and neurotic in personality, she had determination and strength of character. He was prone to periods of depression all his life, and she was the one who urged him out of despondency and into activity. She made sure he was surrounded by inspiration, including shelves of books with color plates such as the insect drawings by Fabre, Chinese manuscripts, and Persian designs. She helped him through writer's block as he was beginning to compose *Mumbo-Jumbo*. She worked with architects and builders to help make La Napoule the artist's retreat that she knew her husband needed.

The creative work of rebuilding La Napoule must have been very satisfying for her. Although architects assisted with the designing of the studio and the arched wall along the waterfront, eventually my mother assumed more of these duties, meeting with the master mason, Jean Cossano, to discuss her ideas for construction and how they might be implemented. She created drawings of doors, windows, arches, and so on, and used watercolors to indicate the hues she wished for details such as leaded-glass windows. My father added the sculptural details: capitals to adorn the columns in the cloisters, overmantels, corbels, and carved doors. The finished buildings, interior furnishings, and landscaping represent a true collaboration.

At La Napoule my parents lived in the style of lord and lady of the manor. Of course, they employed numerous people, giving the town an economic boost. My father and mother designed a park for the town, and an avenue and square are named for Henry Clews. In the manner of noblesse oblige, they sometimes offered entertainments for the local people. On one such occasion, when I was thirteen years old, I was given the responsibility for organizing a fireworks display. Our chauffeur Edouard drove me to Nice to buy the rockets. Then the gardener and I took the fireworks up to the top of the tallest tower and put on a most successful show—despite the fact that we had no previous experience with fireworks! My parents also offered hospitality, food, and drink in the courtyard to the townspeople on holidays such as Easter.

But the focal point of my parents' effort, and the main purpose of creating La Napoule, was to support and enhance my father's creation of sculpture. He and my mother arranged a daily schedule entirely focused on artistic effort. In the morning my father would take his breakfast in his room, make sketches, and read. Starting in about 1932, he would instead spend his mornings writing, and Mother would sharpen his pencils for him (with a knife, as he did not like the mechanical contraption known as the pencil sharpener). Miss Coles would then type up his work, and he would revise, and she would retype. He seemed to rework his writing endlessly! His only published work, Mumbo-Jumbo (1923), was not a commercial success. Then for many years he worked on a lengthy manuscript called Dinkelspieliana. This work is a collection of his thoughts on culture, philosophy, politics, and so forth. Neither he nor my mother made any attempt to publish it—perhaps writing it was simply a way for him to think through his ideas and to express his outrage and frustration about the state of the modern world. I've never read any of it because, I suppose, my mother never showed it to me, and now it seems to have disappeared.

In the afternoon my father would either help supervise building projects or work on his sculpture. My father's studio was sacrosanct, and though I did sneak in sometimes, it was generally off limits to me. It was his private domain, and he kept it locked. He worked there with his two fine pointing assistants: Lorenzo Gonzales and Alfredo Guarnieri. In the late afternoon, he would take tea in the garden with my mother. The two white bulldogs, Tory and Snob, and a variety of birds such as white fantail pigeons, peacocks, ibis, and cranes (he preferred white birds) enlivened the scene. And let me put to rest one myth that has crept into the annals of La Napoule: little silver flutes were most definitely not attached to the wings of pigeons to make a whistling sound! I don't know who first spread this story, but he or she must have been hearing something else!

After tea, my father would typically work on his sculpture until dusk. Then he would join his wife, and sometimes a few guests, for a candlelight dinner. My parents often costumed themselves elaborately when they entertained. At about the age of twelve, I photographed them in their medieval-looking dinner attire, and you can see this picture on the cover of this book. It was in the days before flash bulbs. I had to turn out the lights in the room, open the shutter of the camera, light a vial of magnesium to create the flash, and then close the shutter. Thus a bit of modern technology captured a most unmodern scene.

My father produced a great deal of work at La Napoule, until he became too ill to continue. Still, there has been little critical comment on his work. It seems generally agreed that he was a solidly competent sculptor. Some find his work truly inspired, resembling some of the great moderns in its imaginative and exotic inventiveness. Others view it as merely bizarre. Some criticized his satirical works aimed at society, and some were amused by them. A few of his sensitively rendered portrait busts were judged by Preston Remington of the Metropolitan Museum in New York as "of undeniable distinction… and excellence."

MY FATHER DIED IN 1937 after a long illness. I saw him last in his hospital bed at Lausanne, with a cage of his beloved white birds beside him. After his death he was buried in the town cemetery about two miles from La Napoule. My mother designed a burial chamber for him, according to his specifications, in one of the towers at La Napoule, and that is now his final resting place.

I saw a different side of my mother after my father's death. Though we were separated for a time during World War II (I was in the United States), I saw her soon after. She lived until 1959, a long life, and I feel I came to know her much better than I knew my father, especially after I became an adult.

The end of the war brought to a close a long, difficult period of her life. She had cared for my father during a long illness and during the war had stayed in France (when almost all American expatriates returned to the United States) in order to protect La Napoule and my father's works of art. After the war, though she took very seriously her goal of making La Napoule a permanent memorial to her husband and a center for art and culture, she also managed to have quite a bit of fun.

Although she was a great beauty and appears so regal and serene in the photographs from her youth, my mother was also an adventurous and fun-loving soul. In 1911, she bravely took an airplane ride with the stunt pilot Ruth Law—well before most people dared to venture into the sky in an open biplane. Just before World War II, she asked me to teach her to drive a car, but that effort proved futile. (I'm sure that if the car had had automatic drive, she could have easily mastered it.). In her sixties she wanted to feel the sensation of skiing down a slope, so she stood on the back of my skis as we descended, and somehow we made it to the bottom without a spill. She liked to try new things. The fragile-looking beauty in tiara and lace was not at all faint-hearted.

The memoirs that follow highlight her buoyant personality and gift for vivid description. They capture a long-past era, both in the stories she tells and in the style of her writing. She traces in detail my father's background, sketches in a few details of the early years of her own life, and then concentrates on how they met and the early years of their marriage. She tends to romanticize her marriage to my father, but I think the text also hints at the complexity of their relationship. In one section, she recorded her friend Jelka Delius (the wife of composer Frederick Delius) complaining about how difficult it is to live with an artist, and I sense that my mother agreed. I'm sure that during such conversations, she must have had her own stories to tell.

In reading between the lines, I do find a few things that puzzle me. Though she reports it straightforwardly, as if it was the most normal thing in the world, I do think it strange that my parents embarked on a trip to the United States during World War I, leaving me, an infant, behind in Paris with the servants. I think my mother was anxious to see her two sons in New York, but in doing so she was taking a great risk. The Germans were threatening to overrun Paris at that time—they weren't far away—and if they indeed had done so, it's possible that my parents might have been kept from returning. In that event, who knows what would have happened to me alone in Paris with a nurse and a cook!

But this was one of the many topics on which my mother kept silent. She never spoke to me about this, about her marriage to Robert Goelet, or about her family background. Thus I do value these memoirs a great deal, because they help to fill in some of the blanks. But there is still much that I do not know.

Because the memoirs peter out a bit at the point that my parents begin work at La Napoule, my wife Margaret (who became good friends with my mother) has added an afterword to fill in more details, especially concerning my mother's life from 1937 to her death in 1959. I hope this effort will round out the perception of my parents by visitors to La Napoule. Marie not only collaborated in shaping La Napoule, but also must be given the credit for preserving it so that many people can enjoy it today. Yet she herself is quite self-effacing in her memoirs, so I hope the introduction and afterword will serve to give her her due.

DESPITE MY GREAT AFFECTION for my mother and my respect for my father's artistic accomplishments, La Napoule remains a source of mixed feelings for me. The efforts of my wife, children, and friends in making it a center of art and culture are both moving and inspiring. Yet my earliest memories of growing up there add a touch of dissonance to these positive developments. I recognize the necessity of the life my parents made for themselves in my earliest years—the fact that the creation of art took precedence over everything else—but what is best for the parents is not always best for the child. Because it resonates with the loneliness of my childhood, I have not often returned to La Napoule.

Instead, I did what I suppose all children must do. Building on the good things my parents gave me—opportunities to study, to travel, a certain amount of financial security, and their good wishes—I slowly put together my own life. My father took off in a direction entirely different

Easter 1924 in the garden at La Napoule. Mancha is the boy at right.

from that of his parents, and I have done the same. With a wife who has been faithfully at my side for more than fifty years, three wonderful children and seven grandchildren, and successful business ventures behind me, I can look back on my own life with satisfaction. From the perspective of many years (I am now in my eighties), I can feel a certain sympathy toward my parents and what they achieved at La Napoule. And I hope that their accomplishments and this beautiful spot by the Mediterranean will continue to enrich the lives of many people.

HANOVER, NEW HAMPSHIRE
SEPTEMBER 1997

Marie Clews, New York, 1915

THE MEMOIRS OF
MARIE CLEWS

Henry Clews Jr.

CHAPTER ONE

Henry Clews Jr. and His Family

❧

WHAT QUALITIES ENABLE young people to take up the arts as a career? In our age, when the universal aim is accumulating and spending money, one wonders how young people have the courage and the fortitude to struggle with the uncertainty, poverty, and social disapproval that often go hand in hand with such a profession. Two generations ago in America, no father would look with favor on his son's desire to become a painter, a sculptor, or a writer. "Art does not feed a man," sage parents said. "An artist never grows rich and has little standing in the community. No, my boy, go into business or a bank, into manufacturing or politics—anything you fancy—even the church or the law or the sciences. But don't become an artist. Even the successful ones are regarded as failures in life."

Only a truly brave young person would become an artist after such discouragement. This was especially true in the late nineteenth century, when America was only starting to build art museums and to found its great orchestras. American millionaires were buying yachts and building palatial homes, but they had not yet started to corner the market on art—of which they knew nothing. But eventually they discovered, to their astonishment, that collecting and appreciating art conferred more social prestige than simply owning factories or blocks of houses. Thus, the wealthy came to consider it smart to own art, but not to create it oneself.

Also, according to the dictates of the market, living artists are of far less interest than those who are dead. The market value of works of the deceased can be forced up in a way vastly appreciated by dealers. It is good to be a dead artist, therefore, but never a live one—hardly an encouragement to the budding artist.

There is a legend that a certain destitute and discouraged artist announced his death, grew a beard, acquired a foreign accent, and became a successful dealer in his own formerly unsaleable paintings. He later died (truly, this time) a prosperous and successful old man. This story spells out the situation only too clearly: the artist must take all the creative risks without expectation of financial reward or public recognition, and the dealers line their pockets after the fact.

WHEN, AT A YOUNG AGE, Henry Clews Jr. began to feel a longing to put paint on canvas, a career in art was still considered rather outside the social pale. Thus it was quite natural that his father, Mr. Henry Clews, a Wall Street banker who had won his way to success and a comfortable situation in life, looked with hostility on his son's aspirations. Old Mr. Clews, the founder of the American branch of a respected middle-class family of Staffordshire, England, had struggled too long to get to the top of things financial to want young Henry to take up a profession "unsuited to a gentleman." Instead, he urged him to follow in his own much-respected footsteps to a position of dignity and affluence in New York City.

Yet the Clews family had evidenced artistic tendencies years earlier in England. James Clews, old Mr. Clews's father, had founded a pottery business in Cobridge and had made a name for himself and his brothers with their fine blue-and-white china, stamped "Clews warranted Staffordshire" within a circle surmounted by a crown. They produced a series of historical English castle plates, a Doctor Syntax set (showing the foibles of the simple-minded clergyman, a popular caricature), and a Don Quixote series that had achieved great success in England. For the American market, the Clewses had created plates depicting U.S. historical events, states and capitols, and views of American landmarks.

Old Mr. Clews was careful never to mention that his forbears had been prosperous potters in England and that his cousins were captains in the navy and army. In his private upstairs library, he hid a picture of his birthplace, the family's comfortable English country house in Hilderstone, Staffordshire, near Stoke, England. Called Oxleasows, it stood in a carefully tended park. Also concealed in Clews's private apartments were six or eight family portraits of fine-looking English squires—

some in hunting "pink," some with high stockings and tailcoats—and portraits of ladies in evening dress.

Destined by his family for the ministry, Clews had left Oxleasows for America in the 1830s when his father attempted to set up business in Kentucky and then Indiana. Both ventures failed, and Henry's parents returned to England while he stayed behind in New York. He was pleased by the bustle and excitement of life in America—the battle of brains and energy was open to all who could endure the test. He felt at home in a culture in which the laws encouraged individual endeavor and society venerated rich, successful men, and he never returned to England. He became an American in heart and in spirit.

In the days when Mr. Clews was making a name for himself on "the Street" (Wall Street), it was considered necessary for a man to be "self-made," to have built his own fortune independently (though one friend of Mr. Clews joked, "Well, if Henry Clews is a self-made man, why didn't he give himself some hair?"). Therefore Mr. Clews's ancestors ceased to exist for him, and he never referred to them.

After some years of apprenticeship at various trades, he began to learn the tricks of the stock market and edged into Wall Street in 1856, where eventually he procured a seat on the Exchange. By the time of the Civil War, he had steered his company, Livermore, Clews, & Co., through perilous panics, as the Wall Street kings struggled for supremacy. Always conservative in his methods, Mr. Clews followed the English tradition of fair play, remaining friendly with all parties. Thus his firm stood high among its peers, and Mr. Clews was appointed as U.S. government financial agent for the sale of bond issues to continue the Civil War, which increased his wealth greatly.

But this sturdy firm faced a great calamity when, after the Civil War of 1861–1865, in a desire to help in the Reconstruction of the ruined South, Clews's firm invested in bonds issued by the states of Georgia and Alabama. In 1873, Georgia repudiated these bonds and refused to pay the interest on the coupons, thereby causing a financial disaster for bond holders. Mr. Clews lost much of his personal fortune.

This devastation came upon him at a particularly inauspicious moment. He had up to this point been considered one of the most eligible bachelors on Wall Street. He owned a fine house and drove a coach and four with the finest sports in town, such as August Belmont and William K.

Vanderbilt. He associated with the De Puysters, the Van Courtlands, the Astors, and the Belmonts. Because he had successfully sold government issues of war bonds, Mr. Clews was a frequent visitor at the White House in Washington and often dined with President Ulysses S. Grant.

One evening he had attended a White House ball, a splendid party, and was struck by the beauty of a young lady with whom he danced several times and whom he was fortunate enough to take in to supper. Soon he made up his mind to marry her. Her name was Miss Lucy Madison Worthington, a descendant of James Madison and a member of the old aristocratic family of Worthington, whose sons had held positions as state governors, generals, and jurists. Lucy's father, Colonel William Worthington, had fought with the North in the Civil War, though he was a Southerner. He felt that slavery was morally wrong. He had just been named a general when, one evening during the war, he was accidentally shot by one of his own soldiers.

Before long, Mr. Clews proposed to Lucy. She was impressed by the position of wealth and social prominence that he offered her in New York, although he was much older than she was and his hair was already thinning. She was charmed by his ready conversation on every subject, by his courteous manners and English accent, and by the splendid presents he sent her! When she accepted Mr. Clews's offer, he at once made elaborate plans for a sumptuous wedding and also prepared a magnificent house in New York where she would have every luxury. Then Georgia repudiated its debts, and Mr. Clews, his firm, and many other reputable banks and trust companies found themselves ruined.

It was a bitter blow. Mr. Clews saw his years of hard work swept away, his plans for the future shattered. He sold virtually everything he had and set to work to rebuild his life. For a man in his late thirties, this was no longer easy. The full zest of his youth had passed.

He went to Washington and called on his fiancée. "I am a ruined man," he said. "The repudiation of Georgia's state bonds has cost me millions. I can no longer offer you a place of affluence by my side in New York. You are young and very beautiful and will easily find a younger and richer husband than me. It is not fair for me to expect you to marry me under these, for me, tragic circumstances. I have come to release you from your promise."

Mr. Clews stood before his fiancée and awaited her reply.

Henry Clews Sr.

"Mr. Clews," said Lucy Madison Worthington, holding her chin high, "I gave you my promise to marry you and I will keep it. I will stand faithfully by your side, 'for richer, for poorer,' to the end of my life." The Worthington family traditions would not allow her to reject a man because he had fallen on hard times.

They married in 1874. Instead of a Fifth Avenue mansion with servants to wait on her and a beautiful little brougham at her command to do her shopping, she moved into the Hotel Brevourt in New York, where the new Clews ménage occupied two modest rooms.

Soon the Clews family began to grow: first Elsie arrived in 1874, then Henry Jr. in 1876, and finally Robert in 1877. At the time of young Henry's first memories, his parents were living on East 34th Street near the old Waldorf-Astoria Hotel. Mr. Clews had managed to settle his affairs, pay his debts, and continue his Wall Street operations. In 1877 he founded the firm of Henry Clews and Co., Bankers and Brokers. But although it became one of the most solid and reputable firms on the Street, Mr. Clews never regained the dizzy heights to which he had risen earlier. Yet slowly and steadily, much of his wealth returned, and Mr. Clews purchased a house on Fifth Avenue opposite St. Patrick's Cathedral. Some years later he was able to buy "The Rocks" at Newport, Rhode Island, overlooking the club at Bailey's Beach officially known as the Spouting Rock Beach Association. The actual spouting rock was on the Clewses' property, and Mr. Clews was a founder of the association. He also became a stockholder in the Metropolitan Opera House and purchased Box No. 12, which remained in his possession until his death.

So after some years of waiting, Mrs. Clews came into the kingdom that had been promised her, even if the prospects were somewhat reduced. She was able to furnish her house beautifully and to have an English butler and footman, horses, carriages and coachmen, jewels, fine dresses, and rich friends. Her parties in Newport were all duly chronicled in the press. At the first night of each opera season, Mrs. Clews's diamond tiara was always much in evidence, and her latest Worth dress was typically noted and admired. She had three healthy and vigorous children, and Bridget to help her look after them. What more could anyone wish for?

Mrs. Clews had names for her servants that never varied. All butlers were called Thomas. All footmen were John. The chauffeur's name was always James. No servant dared contradict this Southern lady. She was always decided and dictatorial. Her orders were given with precision and underlined by a wave of her hand. Her friends, too, were careful not to cross her. Only Henry Jr. was permitted to criticize household arrangements, which he did as soon as he was old enough to sit at table with his parents. After he commented on the butler's service one day, for example, his mother consulted her friends who also had English butlers.

"Little Henry is right," they said. "It should be done as he said." Mrs. Clews was flabbergasted. How could the child know such a detail, she wondered—especially Henry, who so often seemed as if he was dreaming? What an uncanny child!

Mrs. Clews loved her son Henry Jr., though with a rather uncomprehending tenderness. She never understood his aspirations to express himself in art and literature, but she loved him and was delighted by his conversation and his observations of the world around him, even at a very young age.

YOUNG HENRY CLEWS'S EARLIEST MEMORIES largely concerned his sister Elsie and the competition that characterized their relationship from the time they were toddling about the nursery together. Both she considered remarkable, unusual children. Mr. and Mrs. Clews were always at a loss as to how to cope with their eccentricities.

Elsie was two years older, and size gave her the advantage at the start. She would take Henry's toys, steal his books, and then fight it out with him. As she grew older, she developed a more cunning tactic: she claimed she was a witch with superhuman powers. Elsie would put on her head a cardboard crown, surmounted by a star (from the Christmas tree) covered with gold paper, and hold a wand in her hand. At dusk, she would flit about the room and decree disasters and punishments on those who did not follow her Fairy Law; transgressors would be visited by ghosts at night. But to those who obeyed the Fairy Law, she accorded privileges, such as reading her books, eating sweets, and borrowing her roller skates.

The threat of ghostly visitations had little effect on Bobby, the youngest sibling, but Henry possessed an active imagination. At night he would awake in terror to find a white-robed figure standing by his bed, and he would scream for Bridget. By the time that Bridget reached Henry's bed, the ghost would have disappeared. One day, egged on by Bridget, Henry decided to have it out with the ghost. He leapt at it and caught a living person in his arms—his sister.

The ghost never walked again, but during summers in Newport, the competition between Henry and Elsie resumed, with tennis matches, swimming races, and diving contests. Both young people were good at tennis and played almost evenly. One day a match between the brother and sister was arranged. Bets were made among their friends—some backing Henry, some backing Elsie. The loser was to pay for ice cream sodas for everyone.

Henry's pocket money was twenty-five cents a week. He always spent it on the first day he received it, treating his friends to sodas and ginger ales at the Newport Casino Tennis Courts. Henry was worried about the bet. How could he treat ten people to sodas? His pocket money for the week was gone. So Henry played this match as he had never played before; the expression on his face was stern, his teeth were clenched, his forehead gleamed with perspiration, and his jet black hair flew about wildly. Amid shouts of encouragement and applause, he won the match, and Elsie had to pay for the sodas.

Later, Elsie found a way to reassert her supremacy. On Sundays, the Clews family went to Trinity Church in Newport. Mr. Clews sat at the end of the pew on the aisle, Mrs. Clews beside him, then Henry and Elsie (Bobby had died at a young age). If Mr. Clews was away, Henry took his father's place at the end of the pew. One such day, Elsie rushed into the church ahead of Henry and installed herself in her father's place.

"I am older than Henry—it is my place."

"No," said her mother, "you are a woman and younger than me. Henry should replace his father."

Elsie did not move. Henry tried to push her out. She sat tight, so finally he sat down on top of Elsie's knees. Elsie pinched him; he pinched her back. Embarrassed by their behavior, Mrs. Clews sent the children home and occupied the pew alone. Later it was settled that when Mr. Clews was away, Mrs. Clews would take the head of the pew.

MR. AND MRS. CLEWS INDEED had two unusual children, both of whom, in different ways, were brilliant. This made them seem eccentric, willful, and capricious at times. Henry rebelled against systems that might be good for other children but that did not suit him.

Henry Clews Jr. was a strong and healthy boy. His hands and feet were unusually small, but his forehead was remarkably high and broad. When he was still a baby, his Grandmother Worthington made him a present of a rocking chair, which seemed to delight Henry so much that he seemed happy only when rocking in it. He would scream if his nurse tried to remove him from it. He remained attached to his rocking chair for his whole life.

The fact that Henry could not take his rocking chair to school, as Mary took her little lamb, was perhaps one of the reasons that he was so unhappy there. He attended many schools: Cutler's, Westminster, and finally Groton. To Henry, the only redeeming feature of these institutions was sports. Football, baseball, swimming, tennis—he excelled at all of them. He won cups and trophies, which he carried proudly home, but he neglected his studies, and his idleness and rebellious spirit had a bad influence on his classmates.

Henry had his own way of learning things. He frequented the school libraries and pored over books of his own choice. He also had long conversations with professors about subjects that fired his imagination. But his classwork was bad.

In Groton, things finally came to a head. "I am not happy there," Henry said to his parents. "Please take me away."

To take a boy from Groton, in those days, was an unheard-of heresy. Hundreds of boys were trying to be admitted to Groton. One had to be "written down" almost at birth in order to be "received" at the proper time. Groton was the destination of boys whose parents were among the guiding spirits of the nation and who were prosperous enough to pay the tuition fees.

The headmaster was Dr. George Peabody, of the celebrated Peabody family of Boston. Everybody stood in awe of him. His reprimands were dreaded; his praise was savored. A boy called to his office would suffer great suspense wondering which would be meted out to him.

Such was the man that Henry Clews Jr. decided to face. It took him a long time to get up his courage.

"What do you want to say to Dr. Peabody, Clews?" asked the housemaster, when Henry asked for an appointment.

"I have something to tell him," answered Henry.

"Tell it to me," said the housemaster. "I'll inform the dean."

"I will tell it to no one but the dean himself."

When Henry finally obtained the requested interview, he was trembling but determined. To himself he kept repeating a phrase that gave him courage: "He can't KILL me. He can't KILL me. He can't strike me dead."

When he arrived at the appointed hour, he stuck out his chin bravely and opened the door to the dean's 'den."

"Well, my boy," said the dean kindly, "what is your trouble? Why do you wish to see me?"

"Dr. Peabody," said Henry, summoning up his courage, "please, sir, I want to leave Groton."

"You are not feeling well, Clews?" he asked, assuming this was the reason.

"Perfectly well, sir."

"Did I understand you to say that you wanted to go home for a while? This might be arranged, if your parents agree."

"I am not ill, and I don't want to go home for a while. I want to leave Groton, sir." The bomb had fallen.

"May I ask your reasons for wishing to leave the greatest educational establishment in our great country?" asked the dean.

"I am not happy here," said Henry. "I do not like Groton, and I want to go away. I am not happy, sir."

"Have you no other reason than that? Happiness comes from doing your duty. You will be happy if you do yours. Return at once to your quarters and prepare your lessons for tomorrow, as you should."

"Dr. Peabody, you would not want to keep in your school a boy who is unhappy here, would you, sir? I do not want to run away—that would not be very brave—but to go away. I wish to leave Groton."

"Go to your room, Clews," said Dr. Peabody, sternly.

Once outside the room, Henry felt almost happy. He had faced the awe-inspiring Dr. Peabody, he had told him the truth, and Dr. Peabody had not killed him—he was still alive, very much alive. He felt his arm. Yes, it hurt when he pinched it, so he WAS alive. Henry Clews Jr. went back to his parents in New York. His father was outraged, and his mother had wept. But what was their displeasure compared to the accomplishment of having faced Dr. Peabody?

Henry Jr.'s education was now provided by tutors. Among them was a splendid young man, Dwight Morrow, whom Henry regarded with both respect and affection. He worked hard under the intelligent guidance of this undergraduate who was helping himself through college. They would talk for hours on philosophy, systems of government, the rise and fall of civilizations, conquerors and dictators. They read the classics and the poets, wandered along the rocks at Newport, and became friends. Later, Mr. Morrow became an ambassador; his daughter Anne married the aviator Charles Lindbergh.

Eventually Henry went to Amherst College, where he proved to be an unruly student, breaking rules and putting the students up to all sorts of pranks. He was politely requested to leave.

Henry next headed for Columbia University, where he became close friends with a professor of literature. But when Henry chose, on on his examination, to ignore the question asked and to write his own essay on another topic, this rather insolent behavior put him in danger of failing the examination and threatened his graduation. This professor intervened for him in a way that put his job at risk, and Henry, not wishing to cause his friend any harm, quietly left Columbia without a degree.

After Amherst and Columbia, Henry determined to try foreign universities and went to Hanover in Germany. He participated in sword matches and also became a skillful fencer with foils. His impish nature took up new mischief—Clews decided to exploit the current fad of spiritualism. By skillful manipulation of black threads, he produced "spirit manifestations" that hoodwinked many, including faculty. But eventually the black threads were discovered and his dupery was exposed. Henry thought it a wise time to move on to the University of Lausanne.

Another sort of trouble awaited him there. He fell in love with a spritely French girl and courted her by night and day until his studies suffered a complete eclipse. Because Mademoiselle Aimée R——— lived in Evian, Henry spent a great deal of time on the steamer that ran between Ouchy and Evian on Lake Geneva. He then threw all pretense to the wind, rented a tiny cottage by the lake, and lived a perpetual honeymoon with the enchanting Aimée.

News of this state of affairs percolated to Mr. and Mrs. Clews in New York. "Lucy, my dear," Mr. Clews said to his wife, "Henry will be marrying that young person next. You had better go and bring him back to responsibility and good sense. You must bring him back to America." Her mission was successful. She routed her son from the "Chalet des Violettes" and turned their steps toward New York and Wall Street.

It was a cruel change for Henry Jr.—from reciting poems to Aimée, to a career on Wall Street supervised by his stern and businesslike father, who, like Lord Nelson, expected all his employees to do their duty.

Henry tried hard to adapt to this new life, which ran like the timetable of an express train. Every minute was scheduled, from his hasty breakfast in the morning to his dash for Wall Street. Henry was good at figures and soon learned a great deal about stocks. From his father he had inherited keen perception and judgment. The idea of achieving power and riches may have tempted Henry in those days; he quickly developed an understanding of investment, the traps and pitfalls of market manipulations, and the motives and intentions of the people around him. His father was impressed by Henry's judgment and even followed his advice on several occasions.

But amid the humming activity of a big office, his days were so fully occupied that there was no room for his dreams. In the depths of his soul, Clews Jr. was not happy, nor did he feel that he had found his predestined occupation. As soon as he got home at night (he still lived with his parents), he would settle into his rocking chair and review the happenings of the day, comparing the advantages of attaining power and wealth with the satisfaction of following the dictates of his inner voices. They beckoned to years of creative work, yet also to risk and suffering—a life without material reward or worldly credit.

Henry was still trying to set his direction as an artist: would he become a painter, a sculptor, a writer? He had never attended art school. He remembered the long conversations with his friends at the university in Lausanne, discussing how they would act as leaven to society, how they would quicken the spirit of civilization. They too had dreams and aspirations and he wished them the best, but Henry was well aware that he had an additional advantage. If he chose art as a career, he knew he would always have a little money in his pocket, owing to his father's comfortable financial situation.

Day after day Henry rocked in his chair and pondered. Then, as often happens, the decision was made for him. His own character forced the issue.

There was a panic on Wall Street—a minor one, but a panic all the same. Stocks went crashing down; values slid toward disaster. In the midst of this maelstrom, Henry Clews Jr. wandered about, suffering acutely for the agonies of those affected by the downturn, frustrated that he could bring them no relief.

"The faces of the panic victims became unbearable. It was as if they were drowning before me and I could not stretch out a hand to pull them to shore and to safety," said Henry later, to a friend. "I became a helpless spectator. The attitude of my father, however, was magnificent. He stood there calmly, like a valiant captain in a hurricane, radiating courage and hope. I had never so appreciated the fortitude of the old gentleman before. He was truly magnificent. But it was more than I could stand, so I disappeared."

After the closing of the market on that day of panic, the firm of Henry Clews and Co. took stock of the situation.

"Where is my son, Henry?" said Mr. Clews, who suddenly became aware that he was not in the office. The staff looked for Henry Jr., but he was not to be found. Mr. Clews then opened the door of a small private room where he kept personal records, letters, and books. Henry was comfortably installed in a big armchair, reading a book.

Mr. Clews quietly walked up to his son and took the book from his hand.

"Shakespeare!" he said. "You can read Shakespeare while the finances of your country totter, while thousands of people are plunged into ruin and disaster? Well . . . my son . . . Wall Street is evidently not the place for you."

Mr. Clews strode firmly from the room and closed the door, not only on his private room, but also on the Wall Street episode of his son's unsatisfactory career.

Henry Jr. never returned to Wall Street.

※

THE NEXT FEW YEARS of Henry's life were difficult, for he had passed from the "opposition" to the benches of self-government. He could no longer be a kicker, a merry prankster like Till Eulenspiegel.

"Facing the great Dr. Peabody was my first declaration of independence," Henry said later on. "I was facing the symbol of a whole system, the product of a complex civilization, which, if good for other little boys, no doubt was not good for me.

"After I won my battle against Groton and against my own family, I was given more freedom to choose my own way. But my father never forgave me for not becoming a Groton man and a Wall Street banker. From that moment on, my father was secretly ashamed of me, although he tried to hide it.

"Life would teach me its lessons, but not from behind bars. I decided that I must choose for myself. Choice is, after all, the greatest freedom in the world. Choice to make mistakes, to work, to become utterly and entirely oneself." Clews made his choice: to seriously pursue the life of creating art.

It was difficult to begin a new profession for which he was entirely untrained. Henry did not even know how to apply paint to canvas. He had to teach himself the long way. His system of learning had advantages, however, for he found himself facing a blank canvas without any of the inhibitions that are implanted in a student's head by masters who, unconsciously, influence students to see life through the teacher's eyes rather than through their own.

Henry took one of the small servants' rooms at the top of his parents' luxurious house and turned it into a studio. Into it he moved his rocking chair, an easel, canvases, and a paint box. His first model was old Ellen, the Clewses' housemaid. After her, he painted the rest of the household one by one, which disrupted the service schedules and annoyed Mrs. Clews. Yet her love for her son made her pass lightly over these transgressions. "I'll rent a studio for you outside the house," she said finally.

So Henry removed his "messy" work from his parents' home and for the first time in his life had a workshop of his own. Few of Henry's early canvases survive, which is a shame, since it is always interesting to study the beginning works of any artist. Henry's lack of instruction made his first efforts slow and uncertain. He had only his eye and his instinct to guide him. He found himself launched in a profession that had no ultimate goal, no finality, no end. The prospects were limitless.

EVENTUALLY, IN ADDITION TO HIS New York studio, Henry set up shop in Paris, a city so welcoming to artists. Yet he still continued to spend holidays in Newport, at his parents' summer home. For Henry, Newport was the scene of artistic inspiration, social hijinks, and the place where he would meet the women who most influenced his life.

Henry's friend Howard Cushing, the painter, lived next to the Clewses' Newport family mansion, "The Rocks." The two used to talk for hours together, sitting on the rocks facing Narragansett Bay, and found that their dreams and ambitions ran along similar lines. Howard had also decided that painting was his vocation and was studying at an art school in Boston. (There is a Howard Cushing Museum in Newport today, housing some of his beautiful, luminous paintings.)

The third artist in this group of friends: Robert Winthrop Chanler, was a giant in stature and splendidly vital. His brashness was a foil to Howard Cushing's refinement and gentleness. Yet Bob had the soul of a true artist and in later years created wonderful wall frescoes, screens, and canvases. These friends discussed technique, compared their canvases, and learned much from one another.

As for social hijinks, Henry had become a dandy in dress and manner. Once he was out of his New York studio and on holiday, the prankishness of his childhood years would return, spurred on by a remarkable person from Baltimore who had appeared in Newport in the late 1890s. His name was Harry Lehr. Aided by Clews and Mrs. Stuyvesant Fish (a woman of unlimited humor), Lehr upset the decorum and boredom of America's summer capital and turned it into a sort of country circus. This group's entirely absurd entertainments caught the fancy of the press and the public.

Mrs. "Stuyve" Fish's house was situated on a slight hill just back of "The Rocks." It was a dignified white colonial edifice with Georgian columns facing the ocean. This house became the center for these bizarre amusements. Mrs. Herman ("Tessie") Oelrichs of "Rosecliff" on Bellevue Avenue, a wealthy widow, also joined in the fun and financed some of the parties.

One of the most audacious events was Harry Lehr's "dog dinner." The well-heeled guests' family pets sat at table, waited on by their masters. A whole series of absurd fancy dress parties at Mamie Fish's house or at Tessie Oelrich's gorgeous Newport "cottage" (including one inspired by tales of Mother Goose) were worked up by the press to appear far more sensational than they really were. Perhaps the height of silliness was the "monkey dinner," at which the long-awaited Prince del Drago turned out to be a very overdressed monkey. In these sallies, Harry Lehr was recognized as the leading court jester to Mamie Fish's sovereign court. Henry Clews stayed in the background, thinking up more nonsense for the Newport society puppets to perform.

Like the other members of this group, Henry enjoyed making fun of society by pushing its conventions and pretensions to the limit. Often he found that society could not tell the difference between elegance and sheer buffoonery. He seemed to spare no effort to cut a flashy figure, wearing white socks, designing his own unconventional waistcoats, and carrying a gold-headed cane. He began wearing a monocle—not to improve his vision, but because he liked how its black ribbon contrasted with his white evening clothes. He also let it be known that he wore mauve silk pajamas and had a white fur rug by his bedside for his feet to touch when he arose in the morning.

Still Henry did pursue more serious interests: his painting and, as it happened, his courtship of Louise Morris Gebhard, whom he met in Newport. The divorced wife of Freddy Gebhard, Louise was recognized as a great beauty. She seemed physically different from other women. Her skin was like transparent alabaster, her eyes deep purple shadows fringed with black, her features as regular as those of the Venus de Milo. In conversation she was amusing, gay, and charming—whenever Clews had the rare opportunity to speak to her. She held the palm in her country as Lily Langtree did in England. In fact they so much resembled each other that there was a near riot in the Waldorf-Astoria dining room when both women happened to appear there simultaneously. Everybody wanted to see which woman was the more beautiful.

Henry and Louise married in 1901 and took up residence in Paris in a little house in Villa Said, avenue du Bois de Boulogne. It was another desperate romance like the "Chalet des Violettes" years before, but this time with an international beauty and a woman of great talent and ability. They were very happy for a few years, and two beautiful children were born to them, Henry Clews III and Louise (who was later to become the duchess of Argyll). Little Louise was called "Wee Louise" to differentiate her name from her mother's. In her baby efforts to say it, she called herself "Wee Ouise," which degenerated into "Oui-Oui," by which she was known all her life.

Clews had by this time acquired a studio in the rue de la Pompe, not very far away. His longing to paint was fanned to a flame in the atmosphere of Paris. At this time, he became friends with Robert Mac Cameron, a Scottish painter who had a great fund of fantasy and imagination. Other painters and writers joined their group and met frequently in Clews's studio.

Clews's wife rather disapproved of these noisy friends, not realizing, perhaps, that her husband was cutting his artist's teeth and really needed contact with other thinkers and artists. To become accustomed to the vagaries and uncertainties of an artist's life, a wife must learn that meal-times will never be respected nor any schedule followed. A man in the flow of creating art forgets the hour, neglects his social obligations. And later on, he likes to rest in his rocking chair and talk over his day's work with his artist friends, who also share their experiences.

To a young woman who merely liked the arts, it was an exhausting job to manage her small household, two children, two nurses, and a cook, while her husband worked at his studio. When he repeatedly turned up at odd hours, smelling of paint and requesting a meal just when the cook had gone out, her aggravation increased. Louise discovered that Henry Clews, painter and worker, was a different person than Henry Clews of Newport, prankster and amuser, dandy and wearer of white socks.

THE DAY CAME WHEN THE Clews family decided to separate. "You are married to your art, not to me anymore," Louise had said. Though this was an exaggeration, in a measure it was true. They divorced in 1910.

The breakup was catastrophic for Henry, who needed a quiet home life, love, and security. He found himself headed for New York, a broken-hearted man. "Oui-Oui" was to remain with her mother; Henry III ("Babou") was to go with his father to America and be brought up in his grandparents' house, with his father living nearby. Under the strain of sorrow and disappointment, Henry suffered a serious nervous break-down and his first attack of depression, which was to pursue him at intervals for the rest of his life.

Henry turned for comfort to his mother. She never said the fatal words "I told you so," but she had always felt that this marriage to one of the most spoiled and beautiful women in the world would not endure.

MEANWHILE HENRY'S SISTER ELSIE was finding her way into an interesting career of her own. She had attended various fashionable young ladies' schools in New York, and then studied at Barnard College, where she took every honor. At Columbia University she received a Ph.D., became a lecturer on sociology and anthropology, and began a distinguished career as an author, researcher, and reformer. These books she signed Elsie Clews Parsons after she married Herbert Parsons. Hers was a valiant and unconventional spirit. She dared to be herself—the new woman. She headed many women's clubs, worked in settlement houses, and advocated women's suffrage and even "trial marriage"!

Herbert Parsons, a lawyer, would later became a member of Congress. He was the kindest and most considerate of men, possessing great integrity. He wholly supported his remarkable wife—her feminism, her anthropological studies, and her long expeditions to study different cultures and peoples. Though she was not an excellent household manager, somehow things got done by the servants, nurses, and tutors. The four children looked after one another when their mother was away. It forced them to be self-reliant, responsible young people.

Mrs. Clews looked with stern displeasure at her daughter's unconventional behavior, but was unable to challenge that keen intelligence and inflexible will. Mr. Clews's attitude toward his daughter combined incomprehension and outrage. He had given her every advantage that a young lady of good family could desire. When Elsie went to Barnard College, Mr. Clews was horrified. No young lady of her position ever went to college. Such situations were meant for middle-class girls destined to be secretaries and schoolteachers—not for the daughter of a wealthy Wall Street banker. Instead, she should be dancing in Newport at parties given for the debutantes of the Smart Set. She, however, preferred to expose what she viewed as the hypocritical and smug social system of her parents' world.

Her first book, entitled *The Family,* upset not only the inner circle of New York society, but also the whole country. It was a very free-thinking book for those days, and many found it profoundly shocking. Mr. and Mrs. Clews were humiliated when, speaking from the pulpit, their Episcopalian priest denounced the book and its "audacious author." He declared it to be the work of an anarchist.

Poor Mr. and Mrs. Clews were utterly crushed and retired from society for some weeks to face this embarrassing ordeal alone. Gradually the subject grew old, and eventually it was forgotten. Elsie's later books were so scholarly that none of Mrs. Clews's bridge friends took the time to read them. Though they passed unnoticed in New York society, in academic circles they received great praise.

Elsie Clews Parsons was a very pretty woman, though she ignored the conventions of dress and deportment that characterized her upbringing. Her skin was freckled from her outdoor treks through every sort of terrain and climate. Rather than skin creams and lotions, Elsie's medicine chest was full of fever pills and remedies for spider and snake bites. Her way of dress could perhaps best be described as a mixed metaphor. For example, she was once seen walking down Fifth Avenue in a very smart black velvet dress and coat and wearing a pair of heavy hobnailed boots fit for the wilds of Canada. No one ever knew if she was aware of such incongruities, or if she simply liked to astonish her friends.

Elsie was ahead of her day, and her pioneering attitude required courage, of which she seemed to have an endless supply. Mrs. Herbert Parsons did not know the meaning of the word fear. "She was so courageous," said an English attaché to the British embassy in Washington, "that I was ashamed of my terror in face of the worst storm at sea I have ever experienced. Mrs. Parsons and I had chartered a sailboat to go to an island near Nassau, when we got caught in a sort of hurricane that threatened to send us to the bottom of the sea. Monstrous waves swept over the boat, carrying away the sails and breaking the masts. We were helpless, and I feared the end had come; so I knelt down in the little cabin to pray.

"Elsie Parsons watched me quietly without a word, her face toward the storm, and smiled with such cool courage and confidence that I felt ashamed and went and sat by her side. Eventually, battered and broken, we got the boat safely into port. What a wonderful woman she is. I take off my hat to her."

CHAPTER TWO

Elsie Whelen and Her Family

❧

DURING THE CHILDHOOD YEARS when Henry struggled with his sister Elsie in the nursery, another Elsie was awakening to life in Philadelphia.

Her father, Henry Whelen Jr., was eldest of four brothers. They were all remarkably handsome—over six feet tall, slender, and blue-eyed, of Irish lineage. Their father, Townsend Whelen, had been a successful banker and broker. Every Sunday, Elsie and her parents, along with her brother Billy and her sister Laura, lunched with Grandma Whelen at her home on Rittenhouse Square. The whole extended family met here every Sunday: the four brothers, their wives, and the nine children.

Henry Whelen was the treasurer and later the president of the Academy of Fine Arts in Philadelphia and subsequently also helped raise money for the creation of the Philadelphia Orchestra. He loved the arts and passed this passion on to his youngest daughter.

"Poppy, if I became a great singer, would you let me sing in public?" asked Elsie eagerly.

"Certainly," said her father, "but only if you were a great artist; otherwise no."

"A great artist," said the little girl. "I must become a great artist. Will you help me to become that, Poppy dear?"

"I'll do all in my power, dear child . . . but look here, you didn't play the accompaniment of this Schubert song like a great artist, I assure you. Now try it over again." And they were off together on the difficult road of art.

Elsie's grandfather on her maternal side was William Spohn Baker, a scholar and a writer who passed his life in art galleries and museums, but principally in the Historical Society of Philadelphia, where he was putting together a series of books and studies on the life of George Washington, including the very comprehensive book *The Engraved Portraits of Washington.* He had toured all the great art galleries of Europe and had decorated the walls of his large, old-fashioned house on Arch Street with fine engravings.

Elsie was charmed by her Baker grandfather and would sit, still as a mouse, in a corner of his study, looking at engravings or reading art books. "Why not associate with the highest, why not pass your life among the mightiest artists and philosophers in the world? Listen to this passage, dear child," he would say, taking down a great volume from one of the shelves. Grandfather would read to her from the poets, philosophers, and dreamers of the world.

Henry Whelen's banking business prospered, and he was able to buy a farm of some sixty acres at Devon, outside of Philadelphia, when Elsie was about twelve years old. During the glorious summer vacations at Clovelly, the name of the farm, life became a daily adventure for Elsie and her siblings. First there was early morning breakfast with Father: eggs and milk from their own chickens and sleek Jersey cows, and heaps of fruit from the garden—strawberries, raspberries, red and white currants, peaches, apples, pears. Then, when the two-seated light station wagon drawn by a spirited roan horse would drive up, all the children would pile in to drive Father to the station, while Snappy, the Irish terrier, followed. Later in the day, they could saddle the two white ponies, Duke and Dandy, and gallop over the countryside.

The happy days in Clovelly drew to an end in a few years, however, for a storm was brewing over Wall Street. The Whelen family, then established at 1724 Spruce Street, decided to close the house for the winter; Elsie's father would live at the Rittenhouse Club, and Elsie, Laura, and their mother would live in Germany for two years. The family atmosphere was overcast. Her mother's dimples rarely flashed in her pretty face anymore.

Although Elsie was sorry for her father, who seemed to have lost lots of money, she could not help but be excited over the idea of sailing away on a big German ship to Hamburg and traveling to Dresden. They could live more cheaply there, and Philadelphians would not observe the changed conditions of the "Henry Whelens."

In Dresden, Laura and Elsie attended Fräulein Bauer's school and had a German governess and music teachers. Life there was a revelation of beauty to Elsie: the opera began in the late afternoon, and concerts were given by great European artists. Her mother bought tickets whenever her allowance permitted. Laura, Elsie, and their governess spent two afternoons a week in the art galleries, admiring Raphael's Sistine Madonna and many other treasures.

The first summer they took a trip through Germany. In Bayreuth, instead of living in a hotel, they had rooms over the butcher shop. They saw Frau Cosima Wagner drive to the opera in an open calèche with four horses, followed by kings of the various German states and other notables. But once in the darkened and hushed opera house, Elsie forgot all but the music. "I want to sing Brunhilde, or Isolde, or Eva in *The Meistersingers,*" she would say afterward.

"Better become a little fatter first," said her practical mother. "Come and have a nice hot chocolate and a bun."

When the next summer came, they sailed back to America.

❧

IN PHILADELPHIA, Laura Whelen became engaged to Craig Biddle. Elsie, who had graduated from the Dana Hall School in Wellesley, Massachusetts, was maid of honor at her sister's wedding. The following year, Elsie's first cousin Violett Whelen was married, and Elsie was again maid of honor. Then, the next year, Violett's husband died, and months later Violett died in childbirth. The life of her son was saved, but Violett's brother Charles Jr., weakened by grief, took a chill at his sister's funeral and died of pneumonia a few days later.

These tragic events threw a shadow over Elsie's own "coming out." She was so overwhelmed with grief by her beloved cousin's death that she fell ill and had an operation for appendicitis. Her right arm became paralyzed following the operation and hung for many months limp and lifeless by her side.

In spite of all this, Elsie was not long dismayed, and her second winter "out" found her dining and dancing every night until her head spun around. She became a very popular debutante, one of the leaders of her set of friends. "Always turn down your champagne glass at table," warned her mother, "so that everyone will know that your exuberance is your own and not stimulated by champagne." One night Elsie, dressed as a sailor, danced a hornpipe on the table of the country club, at a fancy dress ball.

During the summer Mrs. Whelen took her daughter Elsie to Narragansett Pier and then, together with Craig and Laura Biddle, they rented a small cottage at Newport for two months. There Elsie met her future husband, Robert Goelet, one of the most eligible wealthy bachelors in the country, to whom she was married some two years later in 1904.

Their wedding was a beautiful affair, with eight bridesmaids, among whom was Alice Roosevelt, daughter of President Theodore Roosevelt. Elsie wore a white satin dress by Worth, draped with old family lace. She wore a necklace of diamonds and emeralds—a present from her mother-in-law, Mrs. Ogden Goelet.

As Mrs. Robert Goelet, a new, very active life opened before Elsie. Much was expected of her, but she had much to give.

Soon after the marriage, Mr. E. H. Harriman, the powerful railroad executive, invited the young Goelets to go with him and his family on a trip to Japan and China. The party traveled like royalty. They went from New York to San Francisco on a train consisting of ten private cars, a baggage car, a "sleeper" for the maids and valets, and a car for the secretaries and typists, who looked after the business end of the trip, for Mr. Harriman was on an inspection tour.

Elsie liked to watch the great railway magnate inspecting his railroads. There was more force in this little, silent man than she had ever seen before. Later, when she visited Alice Roosevelt at the White House, she watched President Teddy at close quarters and compared the two men. These two personalities became deadly enemies during Roosevelt's trust-busting campaign.

After reaching San Francisco, the party embarked for Hawaii. One whole deck of the ship was set aside for the Harriman party. In a week they arrived. They called upon Queen Liliuokalani in her palace. Her presence was tolerated by the U.S. government, but her power had been reduced to a courtesy.

Next they traveled to Japan. Mr. Harriman's party was received by the emperor in his palace. Elsie and others stayed at the U.S. embassy as guests of the ambassador. The embassy was surrounded by high walls with huge solid gates. Japan had just emerged as victor in the war with Russia of 1904–1905, and the peace was being negotiated by President Roosevelt in Portsmouth, New Hampshire. The situation was tense as the Japanese awaited the outcome.

One night, the ambassador and the Harriman party were dining with the Japanese minister of the interior, who lived on a hill overlooking the city of Tokyo, in a beautiful palace enclosed in gardens and high walls. The news had just reached Japan that a peace had been signed. The Japanese had expected more indemnity and more territorial gains than the treaty accorded them. Crowds gathered in the streets, and resentment was expressed against President Roosevelt. "He has sold us to the Russians," they cried.

Word came to the minister of the interior of a potential threat to his guests. They must leave in haste and regain their compound before the mob marched against the minister's house, for it had become known that Americans were dining there. The embassy landaus were in the courtyard. The ambassador rushed the ladies into the second landau, and the ambassador and the gentlemen led the way into the street. They were preceded by embassy troops on horseback, and officers with drawn swords galloped alongside. Elsie could hear the roar of the mobs, and the roads were bumpy so that passengers were thrown from side to side. "Lie down on the floor," cried Mrs. Harriman. "It is safer so." The ladies crouched down as the landau went rocking through the dark streets. Into the compound galloped the horses; the great gates clanged shut. They were safely inside their fortress.

The Japanese government set a guard around the embassy. Each man was given a rifle and a post to defend. Each woman was given a revolver to use in self-defense.

"Know how to shoot?" asked the ambassador of Elsie.

"Crack shot, Excellency," she said, "won all the prizes, better look out, I'm a danger to all enemies."

By morning, the city was under control.

Mr. Harriman chartered a ship, and his party sailed for China. Unfortunately, because of the aftershocks of an insurrection, the empress dowager canceled her scheduled audience with the Harriman party. However, they did enjoy the sights of Peking and also traveled to Korea before returning home.

❧

ELSIE HAD A BRILIANT LIFE in New York and Newport. She also took trips to Scotland (to Floors Castle, owned by the duchess of Roxburghe, Elsie's sister-in-law), Paris, and Rome. Elsie was becoming a New Yorker, making the usual rounds of parties, but what she loved most was the opera. Box No. 1 was always at her disposal, and she even attended rehearsals to watch Mahler and Toscanini rehearse their orchestras. Enrico Caruso, the great tenor, became her personal friend, and he would sing arias to her as she sat in her box.

She had become, under the guidance of her Aunt Grace Vanderbilt (Mrs. Cornelius), one of the pivots of New York social life. And to the young, gay, carefree set she had added journalists, politicians, and diplomats. This social mix awakened opposition in the family, for a young couple was expected to stay within the bounds of their family's friends. These limitations frustrated her, as did her lack of real involvement in the arts.

No doubt, had she waited for the wisdom of mature years, she might have found a way to weave elements of art and culture into her social life and become a useful figure in many artistic enterprises of New York. But being young and inexperienced, she fretted secretly at the futility of the repetitious round of activities that characterized her young married life. Though Elsie had a big establishment to run and many responsibilities, she had not yet found a role that would give her complete satisfaction. Unconsciously she was seeking an outlet for her abilities.

CHAPTER THREE

They Meet

❧

*T*HOUGH ELSIE WAS NOT EXPECTING catastrophe, it arrived like a tidal wave. Elsie met Henry Clews Jr. at a dog show in Newport in 1910. "Who is that tall dark man with such a large forehead?" Elsie asked one of her friends.

"Oh, don't you know him? That is Henry Clews. He is an artist, you know, divorced from the beautiful Louise Clews. He is living at 'The Rocks' with his parents and little son Henry. He is quite mad and apt to do the strangest things. You had better beware."

It was an unfortunate remark to make, as all danger attracted Elsie. If this sad-looking young man was dangerous, Elsie would brave the danger—and overcome it.

Henry was with his beautiful, exquisitely dressed mother, who spoke to Elsie and introduced her son. He bowed politely and then they looked at each other. It was a long look, full of curiosity and then interest. It was as if they had met before and were meeting again. They were old, old friends from the beginning of time.

Henry's eyes were a mixture of hazel and green. They seemed to be cut like diamonds, with many facets, catching a dozen lights. Elsie felt that he was looking straight into her soul.

There was a brooding melancholy about Henry Clews that set him apart from other men. He resembled pictures she had seen of Edgar Allan Poe . . . the tall slender figure, black hair that made a point on his remarkable forehead, and eyes that looked out into the world, into mysteries and sorrows. He had been deeply wounded by life.

"I want to buy a friend," said Henry, smiling.

"A human friend cannot be bought," answered Elsie.

"A doggy friend can be paid for but not 'bought,' either, and his love is faithful until death. I love these little fellows."

"Faithful until death . . . few can be that."

"Only the great in spirit."

"One can be faithful to an ideal, but how be faithful to the faithless?"

"Some men, like their doggy friends, not only have faith but can be faithful until death."

"Henry," said his mother, "look at this terrier; he seems very gay and affectionate. Would you like to buy him?"

And they moved on.

Later in the week, little Peter, Elsie's second son, was christened. It was a rather solemn party as the bishop had come up from New York and was staying in the house. Mrs. Clews was there, as well as Aunt Grace Vanderbilt and other members of the family. A brother-in-law, the duke of Roxburghe, was godfather. Henry Clews Jr. came in late, carrying three red, blue, and yellow balloons. "For the baby," he said, "with red, blue, and yellow good wishes."

A little later in the season Elsie had tea at "The Rocks" with Mrs. Clews, and they walked down to Henry's little studio over the stable, where he was working on the portrait of a child. Henry was in a white linen painting coat, wiping the Plasticine from his fingers on a towel.

"Do you like the head of that Pierrot?" he said, pointing to a plaster bust. "Pierrot was always the moon-struck lover, the unhappy poet. Here is Pierrot when he believes himself loved; he is in ecstasy, his head is tilted back to see the moon." He pointed to another bust. "Here is Pierrot rejected. His agony is evident; see his thumb sunken into his neck convulsively to ease the pain of his broken heart. It is always so in legends and in life."

He showed her several other sculptures as well. After Elsie had admired them all, they sat down—Henry in his rocking chair, and his mother and Elsie in garden chairs near the window. They talked together until long shadows stole across the room and the atmosphere became electric in the dusk. There was magic, mystery, and sorrow in the air. Imaginative, wonderful conversation flowed and flashed, and Elsie knew she was in the presence of great talent—perhaps even genius.

ELSIE WAS SPELLBOUND. A dangerous potion was working, seeping through her veins, insidiously, silently. She was in mortal danger—not of losing herself, but of finding herself and becoming what she was destined to be. As she sat in the dusk in the friendly studio, she knew this was her home, her spiritual dwelling, her predestined existence. It would bring her world crashing down about her. But Elsie was not afraid.

After many heartbreaks, hesitations, and misgivings, especially her feeling for her sons Ogden and Peter, Marie laid down her life in New York and Newport, left Robert Goelet, and followed Henry Clews. The story of the rending of her life is best left untold, but the story of the building of the legend of Henry and Marie is perhaps worth the telling.

AFTER WEATHERING THE STORM that was necessary before they could begin their life together, Henry and Elsie faced a new world. Henry rechristened Elsie and she became Marie, and remained Marie her whole life long.

The wedding of Henry and Marie took place at No. 12 Washington Square North, in the city of New York, on December 19, 1914, in the home of their friends Bridget and Benjamin Guinness (Marie had been living there with her children). All the Clews family, except young Henry III, as well as all the Whelens and Biddles from Philadelphia, attended the wedding. The ceremony was restricted to the family.

Poor Mrs. Whelen was there, trying to smile and hope for the best. Old Mr. Clews, in a tailcoat, striped trousers, and pearl tie pin, his whiskers dyed a more vivid purplish blue than usual, stood like a pillar of respectability. Mrs. Clews was there too, of course. She had seen her son Henry through many trials and tribulations. With Louise he had experienced a disaster that had nearly broken him. And now he was trying again with another spoiled woman, used to great riches, big houses, fine jewels and dresses, motors, and servants. Was he not heading for a new disaster?

"It will last one month," said the gossips.

"Perhaps six months," said the more hopeful.

"One year at most," said the optimists.

Mrs. Clews had called on Marie the day before the wedding and warned her of all the sorrow and desolation she was bringing upon her son and his family. She had implored her to give up the mad idea.

Wedding of Henry and Marie Clews, December 19, 1914

Marie had smiled quietly. "Do not fear," she said, "there will be no disaster, only happiness and joy and fulfillment. You will see, all will go well."

"She's as mad as Henry," said Mrs. Clews as she drove away in her motor. "God help us all."

Years of love and happiness lay before Henry and Marie, but that was in the future and did not relieve the tension and apprehension of the two families gathered before the clergyman that day. It was Marie's birthday, a day of good omen.

After the ceremony and the timid good wishes of the assembled families, Henry and Marie went to 145 East 19th Street, to Henry's little house and studio where he had lived and worked intermittently, and they stayed there until they sailed for Europe.

When Henry slipped the key into the door, he and Marie found that the tiny dwelling had been transformed into a bower of white lilies, pure and fragrant. The flowers were everywhere, even along the narrow staircase that led to the studio and rooms above.

"White, pure, and perfumed, it is a good omen. Our lives will start clear and fresh as if in a new world. Happy birthday, Marie. This is, indeed, our Garden of Eden without the snake of evil, for I will see to it that no snakes come within our paradise. We will never be turned out of our garden, for we are protected with an armor of light, through which no dark incantation can penetrate. Give me your faith, Marie, and we will enter the portals of our new life hand in hand."

CHAPTER FOUR

Life in Paris

❧

Some weeks later, Henry and Marie arrived in Paris, followed by Marie's twenty-six trunks, and they squeezed themselves into Henry's little apartment in the rue Hégésippe Moreau near place Clichy. Henry had been living in Paris, on and off, for some time, often visiting the studio of Rodin. Henry's apartment comprised two small rooms with a bath and kitchen, facing out on the courtyard. It also had a spacious studio, already crowded with Henry's sculptural works.

Towering among a dozen other works in the studio was the God of Humormystics. Also the tall emaciated figure called The Thinker stood on one leg, among a crowd of other figures and heads. It was like a forest of ideas, with strange, haunting faces that seemed to stare at visitors when they passed by.

In that tiny apartment, the double bed took up almost the whole bedroom, and there were no closets for clothes. Marie's twenty-six enormous trunks, filled with clothes and linen, books and papers—a sort of retrospective of her former life—presented a problem.

"Where shall I put all these?" said the expressman, scratching his head with perplexity when he saw the tiny apartment.

"In the studio, I suppose," answered Henry. "We will make room somewhere."

The trunks were piled up against the wall of the studio, among its plaster inhabitants. "I'm afraid I shan't be able to open them, piled up like that," whispered Marie.

"Do you think you will be able to fit into such a small life?" asked Henry, rather anxiously.

Henry in his Paris studio with the God of Humormystics

"I was wondering if I were big enough to fit into so vast a world," answered Marie, looking at the sculptures.

For months the trunks remained piled up, and the dust of Montmartre and of the studio settled slowly upon them. Henry's valet,

Antoine, whom Henry had renamed Sancho, was much disturbed not only by the trunks but by the advent of their proprietor. (Henry was much taken with Cervantes' Don Quixote; he identified with that character's romantic idealism and in fact called himself Mancha. Therefore it was only appropriate that he should call his servant Sancho, after Sancho Panza.) Sancho muttered under his breath about barbaric Americans who disturbed the life and habits of artists and their serviteurs, who had been happy and fared well when Monsieur was a bachelor.

"Don't pay any attention to him, my dear," said Sancho's employer. "French people are constitutional grumblers. Don't judge them from an Anglo-Saxon point of view, in which people's words are expected to relate to their actions. You will see that these grumblings won't affect the excellence of Sancho's service or of Anna's cooking, and that is the essential, isn't it? They will grow to love you in their own undemonstrative way. You will see." The grumbling of Sancho and Anna failed to throw the faintest shadow over Marie's delight in Montmartre and the romance of her life with Henry. It was *La Bohème* come to life, to be enjoyed to the full.

Paris is the most natural home for art and artists. The city gives them anonymity, respect, understanding, and freedom. No one stares if an artist walks around dressed in a toga and sandals, as did Raymond Duncan, or in baggy corduroy trousers, a flat black felt hat, and a flowing tie. "It's an artist," they say. The Parisians smile with affectionate understanding.

In the evenings, after a long day in the studio where Henry was working on the figure of an old man while Marie sat in a corner reading, sewing, or joining in the conversation with the model, they wandered arm in arm through the streets, sitting down at a bistro to have a beer or merely watching the crowd of people. They would stroll sometimes for hours together, talking, laughing, dining, and even dancing when the music was good.

They mingled with artists, families, lovers, and "little flowers of the evening," as the French call the professional streetwalkers. Both Henry and Marie were a head taller than those about them. Sometimes Henry would buy a few flowers from an old woman with a basket of posies and pin them on Marie's jacket. Both would smile delightedly if one of Henry's old acquaintances from Montmartre assumed that Marie was Henry's latest model.

Marie and Henry in Paris, about 1915

They watched the nightclubs lure tourists into their brightly lighted halls, flamboyant with posters of the latest nightclub queen. Sounds of waltz music and jazz band blended with loud laughter. Sometimes they would see a group of American friends "making the rounds" from café to nightclub. Then they would walk slowly back to their small apartment, the moonlight flooding the silent streets. Sancho and Anna would soon be waking up to prepare breakfast.

"How beautiful it is," said Marie.

SOON, HOWEVER, THEY FOUND THEY needed more room, as Marie was expecting a baby. They rented No. 82 rue d'Assas in Montparnasse, another artists' quarter and quite a desirable location. They moved in in 1915.

It was essentially a well-to-do artist's residence. The famous sculptor

Frédéric-Auguste Bartholdi had lived here, and in the second-story studio overlooking the garden had conceived of and created the Statue of Liberty, which today stands guard over New York Harbor.

The great double doors of No. 82 opened onto an inside driveway, which ran straight through the house to corresponding great doors opposite, which in turn opened onto a little garden. To the right of the driveway was the front door, leading into No 82 and the concierge's lodge, and to the left was a door leading into the four great studios and the apartment of the guardian. Sometimes white-robed nuns could be seen walking in the convent garden next door, and the great convent organ could be heard playing at dusk for evening prayer.

In October, Mancha Madison Clews was born, welcomed by a kind old American doctor and a spic-and-span English-trained nurse, Miss Connolly, who subsequently became a treasured member of the family. Cablegrams were sent to both families in America, announcing the arrival of a baby boy.

Word was also sent to cherished friends, such as William Adams Delano, the American architect. Bill was one of Henry's closest friends, and Henry had made a small bust of Bill some years earlier. When he received the announcement, Bill assumed that the baby boy would be called Henry, too, after his grandfather, his artist-sculptor son, and Henry III, the artist's young son. Bill saw the dynasty of Henrys continuing through the generations. He cabled back in French to Henry the artist: "*Salutations à Henri quatre. Vive le Roi.*"

This message was much appreciated by Henry and Marie, but not by the French Secret Service. Two top-hatted, black-cotton-gloved gentlemen called at No. 82 rue d'Assas and requested an immediate interview with a certain Monsieur Clews, Henri.

Sancho, too excited to remember his manners, rushed into the big back bedroom where Marie was resting with baby Mancha by her side and Henry was in his rocking chair near the bed.

"Monsieur! Monsieur! The Secret Police is after Monsieur," whispered Sancho dramatically. "What will Monsieur do?"

"Show the gentlemen into the salon. I will see them at once," said Henry with a smile. Sancho was aghast at such temerity.

The two gentlemen stood in the hall near the window, top hats in hand. They bowed ceremoniously. Henry bowed in return.

"Gentlemen," he said, "to what do I owe this honor?"

"Monsieur Clews, Henri," said the chief acidly, "we have reason to believe you are a dangerous monarchist and that you are creating a political party called 'Les Henris Quatres,' named after the French king of that name, 'Le Vert Gallant.'"

"Messieurs," answered Henry, "you are under a misapprehension. I am an artist, not interested at all in politics nor in the great line of kings that monarchist France produced in the past."

"But this telegram, Monsieur," said the second black-gloved gentleman, producing the incriminating blue paper from his briefcase, "does it not say 'Salutations to Henry the Fourth, long live the king?' Such a message is seditious, we must arrest you."

"As for Henry the Fourth," replied Henry, "gentlemen, will you kindly follow me?"

Henry led the way upstairs and opened the bedroom door where Marie was resting, little Mancha by her side.

"Gentlemen," continued Henry, with a dramatic gesture, pushing his hair back from his forehead, "I present to you Henry the Fourth and the Queen Mother."

"Monsieur Clews, Henri," said the two policemen, smiling, "forgive us. Is your father also called Henri, there is perhaps too a son of that name?"

"Monsieur, you have guessed the whole secret of the 'dangerous monarchist plot.' We are four Henrys in the Clews family. Will you not drink to Henry the Fourth and his mother?" asked Henry, leading the gentlemen down the stairs to the dining room.

"We would be much honored."

"Henry the Fourth," whispered Marie to her baby. "What a pity your name is only Henry Mancha Madison Worthington Whelen Clews" . . . but little Mancha was unimpressed, for he was asleep.

❧

SANCHO AND ANNA, Henry's old retainers, perked up a bit when No. 82 rue d'Assas was rented. The rooms assigned to the concierge and his wife were large, airy, and opened onto the garden; Anna's kitchen, too, was sunny and comfortable. Still, they had to complain a little. "Rooms on a garden are very damp," objected Anna. "We will all get rheumatism. Madame will see." But in their hearts they were delighted.

"La Mancha" (82, Rue d'Assas, Paris)

Marie's twenty-six trunks were set out side by side in one of the lower unused studios and could be opened when required. And so peace settled on the dwellers, while Henry set up his statues and plaster families in his new spacious studios facing north over the Luxembourg Gardens. They were all that a sculptor required, and so he was happy and went to work with a will.

It was easy to find models in Paris—not just professional models, but little pages torn from the great volume of life, with the stories of their lives printed in full view across their features. When Marie and Henry strolled about in the evening, they often came across such characters. Once they met a Bretonne woman asking for charity. "Come and earn some money," said Henry. "You will have only to sit in a chair and let me make a portrait of you."

This idea pleased the Bretonne, who instinctively made a gesture to her hat as if to straighten it on her head. Clews made a statuette of her like that and called it La Coquette, for she was immensely vain.

Though some of these models' features bespoke tragic lives, others still carried in their hearts happy memories of the days gone by, when they had been loved and cherished. "Monsieur, how can I show my poor body to an artist now, all crumpled and forlorn as I am today? Time was, I lived in a beautiful apartment and had a little victoria of my own. I had a beautiful body then, round and rosy and full . . . but now . . . ah! no, Monsieur, I cannot show you the disgrace old age has brought on me."

But Clews, backed by Lorenzo Gonzales, who worked in Clews's studio for many years as mise-au-pointiste (pointing assistant), and chaperoned by Marie sitting in the corner, succeeded, after several weeks, in getting the clothes off this dear old grandmother and of making sketches and studies of her, which Henry called The Grandmother, The Chaperone, and The Matchmaker.

"They are not ugly, these dear old people," he said. "They are like fine old lace on which life has traced its pattern and design; here are the scrolls, here are the rose patterns. It is delicate and beautiful, to an artist's eye."

One old woman, tall and grim and of evil countenance, was posed as La Tricoteuse. He supposed she would have knitted unmoved in the days of the French Revolution, as the heads of the king and queen of France rolled into a basket at her feet.

❧

MARIE SET ABOUT MAKING a home out of No. 82. She coped with painters and transformed the dark brown and red rooms into pale grays and had hot-water heaters installed in the bathrooms. Then she started furniture hunting in the Latin Quarter along rue du Bac and rue du Cherche Midi. Long wonderful hours were spent in this greatest of all occupations. Robert, her French bulldog, trotted along beside his mistress, rejoicing in all the "doggie" smells of Paris. Marie was filled with similar delight when she found a Louis XV wing chair and had it transported home to be submitted to Henry's critical eye.

Marie also spent days on a stepladder, pasting various shades of silver foil on the salon walls. When finished, it resembled the background of an ancient Chinese screen (made of squares of burnished gold leaf) and threw into relief the vases of flowers, which were the only ornaments.

The curtains, of pale blue and silver brocade, flashed in the light of a crystal chandelier and the tiny crystal wall brackets. The furniture was

Louis XVI, covered with rare old silvered silks; the pale gray carpet had a tiny rim of black. On the chimney stood turquoise blue Persian pots and some jades were arranged on small inlaid tables.

"It needs just a dash of coral," said Henry, half closing his eyes, so Marie went in quest of some ornaments, which would make the color scheme complete.

The third floor was set aside for the occupancy of little Mancha, who had his bedroom on the garden over his parents' room and a lovely bright nursery overlooking the Luxembourg Gardens and the dome of the Panthéon.

A few months after their baby's birth, Henry and Marie sailed for America to see Marie's two sons by her former marriage; baby Mancha, Miss Connolly, Sancho and Anna, and the bulldog Robert held the house during their absence. They sailed on the *Lafayette* (in danger of mines and German submarines, for World War I had begun). On their return trip on the *Lusitania,* the ship was chased by submarines off the English coast, but managed to escape safely into Southampton Harbor. Shortly afterward, however, the *Lusitania* was torpedoed and sunk with all aboard.

Henry and Marie went up to London and prepared to take the Channel boat back to France the next day, as their tickets and war-time permits obliged them to do. But Emerald Cunard, the famous American hostess and a great friend of Henry's, persuaded them to remain in London a few days.

"I'll fix it up about your passport. Johnny in the Foreign Office will manage that."

And so the Clewses stayed over and missed crossing on the ill-fated Channel steamer, which was sunk with all on board, including the Spanish composer Enrique Granados, with whom Henry had had cordial conversations aboard the *Lusitania.* They had met in New York at the première of Granados's opera *Goyescas,* which had been well received at the Metropolitan Opera House. Granados had invited Henry and Marie to sit with him for a short time in the box set aside for his use. It was a little nearer the stage than the Clewses' box, No. 12, which the family had occupied since the early days of the opera.

Marie had left Box No. 1, belonging to the Goelets, where she had enjoyed the opera for some ten years of her life, and was now sitting in Box 12. Old opera-goers had noticed Marie (or Elsie, as she was called in earlier days) sitting beside her new mother-in-law, Mrs. Henry Clews Sr., at the performance of *Goyescas.* "Young Henry" the sculptor sat by his father in the rear of the box, a huge white carnation in his buttonhole.

"She's moved over," said the "Monday nighters," looking from Box No. 1 to Box No. 12.

⁂

THUS, AFTER THEIR HAZARDOUS TRIP from America on the *Lusitania*, Henry and Marie spent a week in London at Claridge's Hotel, which was just around the corner from Lady Cunard's spacious and beautiful house in Grosvenor Square. Emerald invited all of her special friends in London to meet them.

In their rooms at the hotel, Marie found a basket of flowers and a card attached, on which was written, "Don't forget, lunch every day. With love, Emerald."

Officials from the Foreign Office, ministers of the government, ambassadors (if they were amusing) and their wives (if they were pretty), George Moore, Walter de la Mare, the Asquiths, the Astors, Diana Manners, W. B. Yeats, Lord Wimbourne (governor of Ireland), and Thomas Beecham (director of the Covent Garden Opera) were often at Emerald's house. She took the Clewses to the opera in her box and also to a concert led by Beecham, where a young pianist brilliantly played Frederick Delius's piano concerto. Delius had written it in Florida, when he was twenty years old.

It was at Emerald's house that Henry first met Frederick Delius and formed a friendship that lasted all their lives. Both of them were brilliant talkers—paradoxical, whimsical, keen. Henry was delighted to meet an opponent worthy of his blade. Emerald was also pleased and egged them on.

"Why don't you get into the fray?" she would cry to Thomas Beecham, who, thus goaded, added his sharp wit to the conversation. These fascinating encounters often continued for hours.

Beecham was beginning to disentangle Delius's almost illegible manuscripts and adapt them for his orchestra. Little by little Delius's delicate, spiritual, sensuous music became popular in London. Delius Clubs were founded, and recordings were made of his works. He owed much to Emerald and to Thomas Beecham, for Delius himself was shy and diffident in social life and ironic in conversation. Perhaps that sense of irony united Henry Clews and Delius. Both saw the follies of the age in which they lived, the vulgarity and pretentiousness of the materialistic civilizations that ruled the world.

When the week accorded to the Clewses had expired, they took the Channel steamer and returned safely to France. On the way they passed the tragic wreck of the torpedoed steamer they had been scheduled to take, where all the passengers had met their deaths and where poor Granados, too, had perished. Henry took the white carnation from his buttonhole and dropped it into the sea. "A small tribute to a great artist," he said. "May God rest his soul."

In Paris, they were welcomed home. Baby Mancha was fat and rosy, the bulldog Robert wriggled with joy and barked his delight, Miss Connolly appeared sprucely efficient and smiling—even Sancho and Anna were cordial and almost pleasant. "Monsieur and Madame have been missed, food has been hard to find, especially milk for Monsieur Mancha, but we have done our best to keep the house warm and clean. Of course, it was a strange idea to cross the ocean amid shells and torpedoes and go to America in the middle of the war, but each nation has its own ways of thinking. At least Monsieur and Madame are safely back."

"We would like some tea, Anna, please," said Henry. "It was very cold on that boat and train, and we are tired and frozen."

Marie was holding baby Mancha in her arms. He had given her a little smile of welcome, and Robert was cuddled against her feet. "It's good to be home again," she said.

And they took up their studio life once more. Here they spent the rest of the long years of the war, in constant danger of attack. The Germans were only seventy kilometers away, always trying to break through the French defenses to take Paris. At night, when the traffic was stilled, one could sometimes hear the boom of guns (especially the "Grosse Bertha") and see flashes of light in the distance.

Toward the end of the war, nighttime bombing raids became common. At the wail of the warning sirens, Henry and Marie would put on their woolen coats and heavy boots, and, with a flashlight to guide them, would carry their baby Mancha in a basket across the street into the cellars of a ten-story apartment building, a safer refuge from flying shrapnel and crumbling walls than their own two-story house. Robert the bulldog always went along, too, although he was terrified by the raids and would have preferred to hide under the bed.

By the light of candles (all electricity was cut off during air raids), dim outlines could be seen of other refuge-seekers, their children, and their family pets. These neighbors discussed the latest casualties and bomb-struck houses. Their voices and the cries of noisy children deadened the sound of approaching airplanes and the great thud of falling bombs. When the "all clear" trumpets sounded, everyone would tramp through the dark cold streets back to their chilly apartments and warm beds, only to be routed out again, perhaps a half hour later, by another raid, more sirens, more bombs.

Humanity seems to have the gift of adapting to situations of danger, discomfort, and suffering. Parisians got used to the tension of their perilous situation with the Germans at their door; sometimes they ignored the wailing sirens and the crash of falling shells, and stayed snug in their homes. It got to be a sort of sport, next morning, to get from the newspapers the addresses where shells had fallen and to go and see how much damage had been done. In those days everyone was horrified to see part of a house blown out or to read of the death of a few people who lived there. It was just as well the Parisians could not look ahead and see the much greater damage the bombs of World War II would inflict, let alone the atomic bomb.

In their charming house on the rue d'Assas, Henry and Marie had guests every now and then during the war. Henry's brother-in-law, Herbert Parsons, who had married his sister Elsie, stayed in their guest room on his way to join his regiment at the front. He was glad to get a taste of family life, which he loved, and to talk for hours with Henry and Marie. He won the liking and praise of Sancho and Anna for the way he carefully folded his towels after using them.

"*Voilà, un vrai Monsieur,*" Sancho said, with a side glance at Henry, who generally left his towels in a heap on the floor. "One can see that Monsieur le Major comes from a good house."

Herbert's record during the war was outstanding. He commanded troops in battle and was promoted from major to colonel. "With all Monsieur's friends, it is the same," said Sancho. "They all come here as Majors and go home as Colonels."

Frederick and Jelka Delius also would pass a night in town when

Henry with composer Frederick Delius

they had errands to do or when Delius wanted to see the doctor. These evenings were memorable, and Marie regrets that she did not make notes of them at the time, for Delius was a brilliant conversationalist. He spoke of the artists that he had known as a young man in Paris, when he frequented the studios of Montmartre and Montparnasse. Strindberg, Van Gogh, and Gauguin had been friends of his, and he had attended the banquet given to Le Douanier Rousseau by the painters of that day.

Delius had known Strindberg fairly well. Strindberg's pessimism had strongly tinted Delius's outlook on life; both felt that only a few great men carried on the torch of civilization. "These torch bearers," said Delius, walking up and down the room excitely, "hand the flame of art and civilization to each other across the dung heap of humanity."

"Dung is a great fertilizing force, Delius," said Henry. "Even the most perfect lily has sprung from the soil and from the manure around its roots. I admit that genius is rare, but there are so many sorts of genius, so many grades of ability, that are needed to make up a civilization. You cannot push all these lesser but vastly important life factors into the manure pile."

"Dung heap," repeated Delius, warming up, "that is all humanity is," and the conversation would continue for hours.

Delius put all his despair into his *Requiem Mass*. It is the cry of those who do not believe in an afterlife, seeing in death the end of everything. But this secret despair did not prevent Delius from loving life and nature. Some of his songs, short compositions, and orchestral pieces convey a sense of country landscape, water, and wind that make one think a little of both Debussy and Grieg. Yet they are distinctly like Delius in essence.

One evening as the Deliuses were visiting, the air raid sirens wailed and screeched, and shells began to fall. There was no time to get to the shelter next door, so the Clewses and the Deliuses sat together in the darkened library and watched the air battle through the glass bay window that overlooked the Luxembourg Gardens. It was a wondrous but terrifying sight. German planes were trying to bomb the city, and French planes were fending them off. One plane fell to the ground in a great sweep of blazing light, and another was heading straight for the Luxembourg Gardens—bang, bang, roar, crash! Had it fallen on the house? No, just next door. Fire was springing up. "Jelka," said Delius, "carry my manuscripts to the cellar, I don't want them to burn. Marie will show you the way. And you, Clews, you can't carry your big works, of course, but why not take down those statuettes I admired this afternoon?"

And so they all four went to the cellar, which afforded scant protection, until the "all clear" was given and the bugles blew. "Better get a little sleep until the next raid," said Clews. "We are used to this most nights, but you are used to country calm and nightingales." The next morning, all the windows of the studio were found to be broken. "Where shall I find the glass to repair them?" said Sancho despairingly. "There is no more glass in Paris, Monsieur, no more glass." But he managed to find some, in the French way.

Sometimes Henry and Marie would spend a weekend with the Deliuses at Grez sur Loing, just beyond the Fontainebleau Forest. The house was roomy and picturesque, but did not have what the French call "*le confort moderne*" or electric light. Delius's music room was commodious and had several upholstered chairs, for, being an Englishman, he liked to lounge in chairs and flatten out at least the last two vertebrae of his backbone. There was also a beautiful Bechstein grand piano. Over the piano hung a great painting by Gauguin, called Nevermore, which Delius had purchased from Gauguin personally when the painter was so hard up that he was hungry and despairing. Delius had bought it for practically nothing "for I wasn't rich myself, either," he said.

Delius had an uncle who was very generous to him and who finally left him enough to live on comfortably.

Jelka was often in the kitchen, helping to prepare the lunch with one *bonne à tout faire,* which was all they had. Though Norwegian, Jelka Rosen had grown up in Germany, where her father had been courtier to a grand duke and grand duchess. Jelka would reminisce about court etiquette: When an invitation came from the court to attend a dinner or a ball or a tea party, the messenger who delivered it into Mrs. Rosen's hands would say, "A small party this time. I think the *Gnadige Frau* should wear her green dress with lace." Or when it was a ball for visiting royalty, he might say, "The *Gnadige Frau* should wear her silver brocade and her diamond ornament."

Although Jelka herself was an artist and produced fine paintings, she would paint only when Delius was composing and the housework was finished. When Fred was ill (he eventually went blind) and out of sorts, Jelka's life could be very unpleasant. "I often say I can stand it no longer," she would say, "that I must go and let him get on by himself. But then"—and her face would suddenly clear—"where would I ever meet again so great a musician, so wonderful an artist?"

Sometimes Delius would play some of his songs for Marie, to see if she liked them. If they were low enough for her voice (she was a contralto), she would sing along. He praised her musical comprehension and phrasing, but did not think her voice adequate in strength for the concert stage. "You might have sung my songs for me. You understand their spirit," he said regretfully.

In Jelka's studio was a gray pigeon in a cage, which had come to the Deliuses' house one night in a storm and tapped on the window. He had hurt his wing and needed shelter and help, and he became a great pet.

Several months later, when the Clewses were at Grez again, Marie asked after the pigeon, as she saw his cage empty. "Oh!" said Jelka, slightly embarrassed, "well, you see, we could get no meat at all for several days owing to the war . . . and . . . well . . . Fred needed nourishment . . . so we ate him."

Marie stood transfixed with horror. Eat a pet! A little bird that had tapped at their window and asked for help! It was pure cannibalism. "I suppose you would cut off your right hand and cook it if Fred needed it," said Marie indignantly.

"I suppose I would," answered Jelka modestly.

As the Germans got closer to Grez, the Deliuses decided to leave the area to find safety. Delius made a point of hiding his wine so that the Germans would not get it. "One of these days they will break through that line and in an hour they will be drinking my precious wines." Henry and Marie helped transfer the bottles under the floor of a little tool house in the garden. "They will never look here," said Fred.

"And what about your Gauguin, you won't leave that behind?" Henry looked with admiration at the beautiful golden nude figure of a woman lying on a couch.

"I will have to sell it one of these days," said Delius sadly, "for my funds are running low and the war goes on forever."

When the Germans did finally overflow the Fontainebleau Forest and Grez sur Loing, Delius left with a valise and the Gauguin rolled on a stick under his arm. He and Jelka endured terrible traveling conditions and suffered many privations. But after the armistice, when they got back to their little house (which they found in deplorable condition), they unrolled the Gauguin and put it back in its frame. Then they dug up a treasured bottle of Bordeaux and celebrated.

DURING THOSE FOUR YEARS OF WAR spent in Paris, Henry and Marie suffered from the lack of many things and from the cold. The studios were big and hard to heat, and because coal was rationed zealously it was hard to keep up an adequate supply. But resourceful Sancho was able to fix things up with a friend of his, and he got bags of coal smuggled into the cellar by night.

"I know it's all wrong," whispered Marie to herself, "but I must keep Henry and baby Mancha warm. I suppose it's like killing the pet pigeon so that Delius might have a meal." She pressed rolls of bills into Sancho's hands, and the house became tepid—hardly warm, but at least livable.

Henry and Marie Clews with his daughter Louise, their son Mancha (on Marie's lap), and servants in the garden of "La Mancha," 82, rue d'Assas, spring 1917

All the same, the Spanish flu (also called the black grippe) descended on the household as it did on nearly every house in Paris. Everyone was stricken except Henry and Marie. They remained afoot, Henry in his studio and Marie left to look after the whole household, including Nou-Nou (Mancha's nurse) and baby Mancha. This terrible sort of influenza that fell like a plague on Paris. It struck suddenly, and immediate treatment was imperative to prevent death. Doctors and nurses were overworked, and many Parisians died.

Luckily, Marie managed to get the dear old American doctor who had brought Mancha into the world, and devoted Miss Connolly came to "her baby's" assistance. Between them they saved little Mancha's life, but it was a close shave, and the threat of the grippe cast a dark shadow over the little household on the rue d'Assas.

When Sancho, Anna, and Nou-Nou had recovered, Marie found herself ill with exhaustion and shock.

"We must get away," said Henry. "You need a change of air. But how can we manage to get permits to leave and places on a train to Switzerland?"

The permits were finally obtained, and Henry and Marie went to Lausanne to the Hotel Beaurivage, which was always a haven of rest from the storms of life. While they were at the hotel, enjoying the lake and the mountains and breathing in the pure fresh air, a short middle-aged woman, dressed in black, approached them.

"I am Netta T———," she said, with a sweet but sad smile. "I am your old childhood friend. Don't you remember me, little Netta on Bailey's Beach? Henry, you must help me. You were always a chivalrous little boy. I am in trouble. Will you be my Knight Errant, my Don Quixote?"

Henry eventually found himself fighting to help Netta extricate herself from a terrible situation. She was one of the immensely rich American women lured into marrying a European aristocrat in need of cash, to regild the family coat of arms and repair the castles. Her husband, young and attractive, belonged to a family prominent since medieval times. He had gained control over her money and then drove her out of her home in Florence, separating her from her two daughters and placing her under the surveillance of a terrible "trained nurse" (in reality, a jailer). He had managed to do this by paying doctors and lawyers to certify her as insane while she was traveling in Switzerland to improve her health. Henry and Marie knew that, though Netta might be considered a little peculiar, she was certainly not insane.

Netta's letters asking her own father and family for assistance remained unheeded, as her husband had told them not to heed her "illusions" and imagined persecutions. The war made it impossible for them to reach Switzerland anyway, and poor Netta, in the meantime, was beating her head against the bars of her cage.

Henry discovered that a paper had been filed with the authorities that made imperative her forced residence in Switzerland under the "surveillance" of a nurse. The first thing to do was to have the paper rescinded. This was a difficult matter because the doctor who had signed the certificate, the lawyer who had drawn it up, and the authorities who were pledged to keep it operative had all been generously paid for their trouble.

Cables were exchanged between Henry and Netta's family. After a long fight, they finally got the paper withdrawn and discharged the "jailer" nurse. Then, under the guidance of a friendly Italian senator who was also a lawyer, the poor countess was able to return to Florence and be near her daughters. To accomplish this, Henry and Marie spent many weary hours with doctors, lawyers, and officials. They even had to go with Netta to the insane asylum in Geneva to have her certified as sane.

Later on, Netta gave Henry a gold cigarette case on which was engraved: "To Henry, my childhood's friend, to you, O Don Quixote, who comforted and freed the oppressed. Netta." It was his sole reward for his trouble. It was all he wanted.

CHAPTER FIVE

La Napoule

❧

WHEN THEY LATER needed to escape from Paris for another short rest, Henry and Marie decided to go to the south of France. They procured permits to travel. After a long and tedious journey in day coaches, with a crying baby and a disgruntled nurse, they reached the land of sunshine, clear blue sky, peace and quiet, waving palms, and orange blossoms. It seemed too good to be true. After a month of rest and recuperation at the Hotel du Cap d'Antibes, these two refugees from Paris started house-hunting along the coast.

The house agent had said, "Well! there's La Napoule, a broken-down so-called château where Daisy, princess of Pless, used to live. It's been empty for years, nobody likes it, nobody wants it. You might go and have a look. It has high walls and towers."

"Please give us the keys. We will go and see it," said Henry and Marie.

Along the high road on the edge of the Mediterranean from Cannes westward to La Napoule, they rode in a hired victoria drawn by two horses. The region was desolate, with sand dunes and umbrella-pine forests. Not a cart or wagon was on the road. The silence was broken only by the sound of waves on the pebbly beach.

"It is a bit lonely," said Marie.

"Solitude is what I need," answered Henry, "aloofness, a hidden corner to be alone with my art, away from humanity."

As they approached the village of La Napoule, the old castle with its two Saracen towers grew up before them. A high wall enclosed the gardens and a fringe of tall pines along the sea, breaking the salt breeze. One could catch glimpses of a stone house surmounted by a red tiled mansard roof and monstrous brick chimneys.

The cab drew up before the iron garden gates of the château, and a guardian opened the doors to this forsaken paradise. The driveway was bordered by tall eucalyptus trees. Even at first glance Henry and Marie felt an atmosphere of silent mystery, as if a spell lay over the place. Hand in hand they walked down the allée toward the house. The eucalyptus trees were immensely tall and met at their tops, forming a vast cathedral aisle. Strips of bark were peeling from their mottled green trunks. The driveway was spattered with slender yellow leaves and exquisite dusty gray–green eucalyptus seeds, which had a delicious odor when pressed between the fingers. Marie put one in her pocket for luck.

The allée led to a courtyard that was distinctly disappointing, except for the two Saracen towers that flanked the L-shaped wings. The central structure had been modernized in the worst pseudo-Renaissance style, and the gigantic red brick chimneys were eyesores. The two-story west wing had served as a cowbarn. The east wing had been a stable and coach house. Both wings were dilapidated and ugly. To make matters worse, a solitary palm tree stood in the middle of the courtyard, caged in by red geraniums.

"The burghers have had a free hand here," said Henry with disgust.

"We could liberate the palm tree," answered Marie hopefully.

The central structure was worse than the wings and the courtyard. The main corridor was crossed by other corridors. Along the sea front were two salons and a dining room papered with flamboyant stripes and bunches of flowers. The corresponding three rooms above were bedrooms; the center one, obviously Princess Pless's bedroom, was decorated with wallpaper of pink roses, a pink carpet, and pink stuffed furniture. It was a bourgeois paradise.

But the view from this room's balcony was so beautiful, the Clewses forgot the meanness of the suburban villa. The whole blue Mediterranean lay before them: the bay of Théoule to the west, enclosed by a chain of curving hills; Cannes to the east, shimmering in the sunshine across the bay of La Napoule. The Iles de Lérins studded the sea like two green lily pads. Henry and Marie could see the layout of the old château from this vantage point. The remains of a round tower and vestiges of fortifications, built on rocks that dropped sheer into the sea some fifty feet below, enchanted them.

"It must have been beautiful, even grandiose, in the old days," said Henry.

"There is a sand beach down there for little Mancha to play on, but only one bathroom for all of us and the baby."

"It is aloof, it is surrounded by walls, and the Saracen towers are still magnificent. Let's take it for the summer."

"But with an option to buy, in case we like it."

❧

AND SO HENRY AND MARIE, with baby Mancha and Nou-Nou, moved into the villa-château of La Napoule for the summer. They arrived one day from the Hôtel du Cap d'Antibes in a taxicab, with Henry's rocking chair tied to the roof.

This chair was his most precious, most essential possession. When he traveled in a train, his rocking chair went along in the baggage car. When he went by motor, it was fastened to the roof of the car. All of his friends knew of this peculiar mania. "There goes Clews in that car, didn't you see his rocking chair on top?" As soon as Henry arrived at his destination, the chair was set up and he would begin to rock. Henry said that rocking put him in touch with the cosmic forces of the universe. The motion of gentle swinging not only calmed Henry, but also induced a sort of reverie that liberated his subconscious. Once Henry's rocking chair was set up and he started to rock, everything else fell into order. All Clews's ideas came to him as he sat alone, rocking in his studio, or early in the morning in bed, half awake, half in the world of dreams.

Later, down from Paris came Henry's two faithful retainers, Antoine (Sancho) and Anna Milleraud, who knew all the rituals of an artist's life. They brought the nightingale and Robert the bulldog. When little brindled Robert saw his master and mistress after more than a month's absence, his joy was so great that he leapt into their arms, yapping with delight. Then he started to run in circles to express his happiness. Around and around he went, faster and faster. Suddenly he dropped at their feet. His valiant little heart had burst with joy.

"What a beautiful death—to die of love," said Henry softly, turning to console Marie.

But she held Robert's poor limp little body in her arms and would not be comforted. Robert had been always there, always a member of the little family. When Nou-Nou, dressed in her cape, long black lace veil, and gold hoop earrings, walked in the Luxembourg Gardens pushing little

Taxicab with Clews family and Henry's rocking chair en route to La Napoule,
May 1918

Mancha in the shiniest pram in Paris, Robert walked sedately beside them to keep away stray dogs and to growl at policemen who approached too closely to better observe the attractive Nou-Nou.

"Oh, Robert, dear little friend, how could we have gone away without you. Forgive us, Robert, we did not know of your great love for us nor of ours for you."

And Marie wept and wept—the first of many love tears shed at La Napoule. Robert was buried under a blooming oleander bush in La Napoule's enclosed garden.

❧

HENRY AND MARIE spent the summer of 1918 at la Napoule in the villaized architectural eyesore the bourgeois had made of a once-noble château-fortress.

"Just what do you mean by the word *bourgeois,* which you use so often?" Marie asked Henry one day.

Marie with Robert, who died of love

"Well, the bourgeois are those who possess only a group identity and have lost individuality and freedom of judgment. This tendency has become accentuated since the Middle Ages and is especially rampant now, owing to the tyranny of the daily newspaper and the radio. Only the very great thinkers of today dare to differ from the crowd. The majority think and act along a middle course, bereft of imagination. I suppose they feel more comfortable in their middle-class conceptions, which extend to their houses, their furniture, their morals, and their thoughts.

"This old place was built for defense and had a stern and magnificent appearance, with crenellated watchtowers and high walls. All the villagers of Napoule came here when under attack, just as we go into underground shelters during air raids today. But look what the burghers have done to this dignified house—reduced it from a château-fort to a villa with a captive palm tree.

"See those monstrous brick chimneys over our heads? When the burgher tries to add frills to his 'essentials,' he becomes pretentious and ridiculous. He is incapable of fancy and imagination, for beauty is a quality of the spirit."

"If we buy this house, we will have to take down those chimneys," said Marie.

"And build a studio for me," Henry answered.

Thus the idea of reconstruction crept into the minds of these two Americans. They would eliminate the ugly and pretentious, they would construct the harmonious and the beautiful. Had they not made their house at No. 82 rue d'Assas into a dwelling as exquisite as it was unusual? Had it not begun to glow and to bloom through the efforts of the artist Henry and his collaborator Marie? In the end, La Napoule won out over Paris. Henry and Marie decided to buy the château that had so bewitched them, and which was to hold them enthralled for the rest of their lives.

BACK IN PARIS the family prepared for another long cold winter of bombing and shelling. They planned to move south in the spring. On the morning of November 11, all the whistles, sirens, and church bells of Paris began to scream and ring together. "Another raid," said Marie. "Let's get baby Mancha into his warm clothes and carry him to the cellar." But the din increased and no bomb explosions were heard . . . people began running out into the streets to see what was happening. Suddenly a great cry arose. It seemed to come from everywhere at once—from the houses, from the sky, from the streets. "Armistice! Armistice!"

When everyone was sure it was true, quite true, mad joy spread over Paris. People rushed into the streets, kissed each other, danced, and sang hysterically. Military bands marched down the Champs Élysées. The four years of horror, anxiety, death, and hunger were over. Paris had withstood attack. General Gallieni had halted the enemy on the Marne and Paris had never been taken. "Armistice!" cried Paris, and everyone danced until they dropped, exhausted with relief and joy.

⁂

MARIE'S FRIEND William C. Bullitt, an American delegate to the Paris Peace Conference after the armistice, would bring news and political gossip to Henry and Marie. Bill (a neighbor of Marie's when she lived outside Philadelphia) was becoming sympathetic to the Communists; after being sent by President Wilson to Russia to investigate the effects of the Russian Revolution, he recommended early U.S. recognition of the new Russian government.

Henry had been deeply shocked by the horrors of the Russian Revolution. He abhorred the bloody upheaval, the murders of the imperial family, and the unjust imprisonments and cruelties visited on innocent people.

After dinner, the conversation on the subject of Bolshevism became so heated that Bill left the house in a huff, and Henry had to send his hat and coat after him down the street. They did not see William Bullitt again for decades. Much later, years of ambassadorship to Russia changed his enthusiasm for Communism.

⁂

IN JUNE 1919 the Clews family moved for good from the rue d'Assas to the sunny coast of the Riviera, where a new and constructive life awaited them. The deeds had been signed before the armistice, but they did not move until June 1919, when the weather was warm.

Transporting a whole studio from Paris to La Napoule was a Herculean job. They also had to move furniture, baby Mancha and his toys, Sancho and Anna (who at last had something real to grumble about), their precious library of books, the turquoise blue Persian pots, and their Turkish rugs. Great vans swallowed up the house's treasured contents. The mandarin ducks that had sat so majestically on the turquoise mosaic pool Henry had built in the garden were sent to the zoo, and the turtledoves were given away.

"The moving man says he must have Monsieur's rocking chair, or he will close the van and it will be left behind." And so Sancho pushed Henry's rhythmic liaison with the stars into the van, and the doors

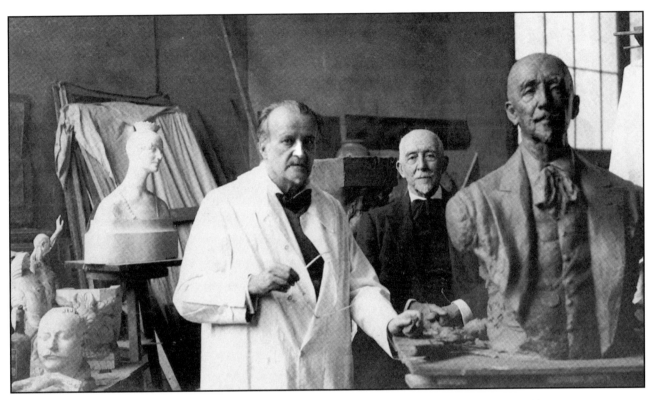

In the studio at La Napoule with le Comte Gauthier-Vignal and Henry's bust of him

banged shut. The spell was broken. No. 82 rue d'Assas was no longer "La Mancha," Henry's home. His rocking chair had gone.

LIFE IN LA NAPOULE was anything but comfortable at first. Only one bathroom was shared by everyone. For an American family, this was disastrous. Fitting into the too-small living quarters made everyone cross, and Marie sometimes regretted leaving the spacious house on the Luxembourg Gardens. The drab ugliness of the "burgher's dreamhouse" was impossible to escape. But worst of all there was no studio . . . and all Henry's plaster figures, easels, revolving stands, and other equipment were placed in an old stable that still had mangers for horses and cows.

And that solitary palm tree in the center of the courtyard, caged by brick red geraniums! Marie ordered its execution.

Henry set up his rocking chair and one of his sculpture stands in an outbuilding, but the light was bad and he did not feel like working.

During a three-month period when Henry went to America to visit his son Henry Clews III at school in Arizona, Marie set about building a studio along the west side of the courtyard. Since she had not yet assumed the architectural duties of La Napoule, an architect was found and a great studio came into being. Henry's treasures unfolded their wings and hopped back into their accustomed places. There was a splendid north light, and heat was produced by the same big stove that had warmed the studios in the rue d'Assas.

This studio was almost completed by Henry's return. Mr. Gonzales, Henry's pointing assistant, came down from Paris with his wife and daughter and took an apartment in the village. Under his guidance, everything slid back into place and Henry began to work again. His happiness and comfort were the basis of Marie's existence and so she began to feel more at home in this broken-down château.

CHAPTER SIX

Mumbo-Jumbo

*D*URING THE LONG hot summer months of l922 at La Napoule, before the studio routine had been reestablished, Henry began to write a book. Marie moved a bridge table, a comfortable chair for herself, and big pads and pencils into the studio. She allowed plenty of rocking-room for Henry in his chair opposite her. Then the work began.

Henry had the common phobic reaction to an empty page. He tried to comfort himself by thinking of other writers who had had similar difficulties (Maupassant had to have a chair on his right side, to keep from falling into space; Balzac had to have lighted candles all about him). To get him started, Marie struck a bargain with Henry. She would go to Nice in their little car, take with her Henry III (who was visiting), and do some shopping, if big Henry would promise to write half a page of something—it did not matter what—on the big white foolscap page she set before him.

On her return from Nice, he was jubilant. "I've written my page," he said. "Listen to this." And he read out the first page of *Mumbo-Jumbo*. Then the real work began. Henry would rock and dictate, Marie would write and suggest. The hours flew by and the work progressed. It was absorbing. The plot began to take shape, each character was discussed and analyzed, the dramatic action was weighed. The pitiful character of Mervyn, the simple-minded artist exploited by clever art dealers, was treated with sentiment and tenderness. The rest of the work was hilarious. Henry and Marie would laugh full-heartedly at every absurd situation. Once begun, the book required no great effort; it unfolded delightfully before their eyes. Both were disappointed when it was over.

Grant Richards, the English publisher, was in the neighborhood and came to read the manuscript. Henry and Marie were on tenterhooks and could scarcely manage to sleep or eat, wondering what he thought. At the same time they tried to appear unconcerned. Grant Richards took the manuscript to London, accepted it, and put it to press at once. *Mumbo-Jumbo* was published in England in 1923 and aroused roars of laughter in the press. The London papers were enthusiastic. Here is a sampling of their comments:

THE BYSTANDER: "If you want to read the most turbulent, hot-headed, white-heated Philippic ever directed against modern cant and hypocrisy, plutocratic pretensions, democratic stunts and neurological art, I advise you to read Mr. Henry Clews' book *Mumbo-Jumbo*.

THE EASTERN MORNING NEWS: "The idea of the satire is gorgeous and it is gorgeously carried out. The reader has to thank him for making him laugh more wholeheartedly than he has laughed at anything he has read for ages."

THE OBSERVER: "America, with her machine-made civilization, graft, 'highbrow' literature, commercialism, and snobbery, is attacked in a tornado of condemnatory adjectives. Nor is English literature spared, H. G. Wells and G. B. Shaw being particularly singled out for castigation which is the more remarkable as Mr. Clews' introduction is conceived quite in the Shavian spirit."

THE TIMES, LONDON: "The subject matter of the book is a protest against democracy and incidentally against Mr. Bernard Shaw. And the humor of it in the present case is that Mr. Shaw is attacked with his own weapons. Mr. Clews, Jr. has taken for his model an even greater authority than Mr. Shaw. He has gone to Rabelais."

The author of Mumbo-Jumbo *at work*

THE MORNING POST: "Mr. Clews has a prophet's rage . . . when he at last comes to the play . . . it must be confessed that he does it with remarkable skill, originality and distinction."

GRANT RICHARDS sold the American rights to Boni-Liveright. Before printing it, the publisher had an interview with Henry and Marie in New York in 1923. Henry's father had just died, and Henry and Marie were in New York for the settlement of his estate. Mr. Liveright wanted Henry to make some changes in his work.

"*Mumbo-Jumbo* is a good book, Mr. Clews, and can become a best-seller if you will agree to a few minor changes—some criticisms of people whose works you excoriate with such glee, little changes in the characters . . . very unimportant to you, but important to me and to the universal success of the book." The publisher then mentioned a few specific changes.

Henry was adamant. "I would prefer not to change a word," he said.

Marie wished to temporize. "Let us examine carefully what Mr.

*Servants in ceremonial costumes designed by Henry, on the occasion
of the laying of the cornerstone of the studio at La Napoule, spring 1920*

Liveright means," she pleaded. "Some small changes would not alter the
sense of the book."

Henry thought it over, and, in spite of Marie's pleading, he refused to
change a line. *Mumbo-Jumbo* was published as it was. The press in
America treated *Mumbo-Jumbo* differently than the English critics.
London criticized the book; New York criticized the man. These critics
could not forget that Clews was the son of "one of America's most distinguished bankers." They ladled up a good deal of class criticism. Also,
Henry had dared to expose the weak spots in the democratic system, and,
since democracy is practically a religion in America, his treatment of it

was hotly resented. Still, reviewers also included a good deal of praise in their critiques.

Francis Hackett, in *The World,* called Clews "the great American kid, a literary dude" and accused him of "using living people under thin disguise," stating that "his technique of these portraits is, on the whole, better than 'Town Topics' [a society column]." He said Clews had "deficient taste" and that his English was "journalesey."

The *New York Herald* said, "New Clews satire finds world awry . . . financier's son invents words to aid in denunciation of nearly everything."

The *World of Books* wrote: "Son of financier practices the gentle art of brick-throwing. From B. Shaw to C. Sandburg, all is vanity . . . the very book this summer for the hammock, but mind you, don't set the chocolates too near it."

The *New York Telegraph* states, "Whatever his purpose, he has wrought cleverly, so cleverly that we associate his work with that of Cervantes and review *Mumbo-Jumbo* with recollections of Don Quixote."

The *New York Tribune* hit Clews from a class point of view: "During my many years of reading, I recall no work so silly and sophomoric, vulgar and illogical, cheap, strident and idiotic. *Mumbo-Jumbo* is merely the first literary effort of a man who has been misled into a belief of his own omniscience, elegance, power and refinement by the fact that his butler bows and says 'Sir' to him . . . Mr. Clews is not intellectually mature. His butler's obsequiousness has stunted his growth."

The *Newark Evening News* resumes: "*Mumbo-Jumbo* mocks with Rabelaisian wit and humor the weakness, folly, above all the stodginess of the contemporary radical. . . . His book is not only to be read, but to be reread."

The *New York Times Review,* April 22, 1923, gives the most complimentary and witty criticism of *Mumbo-Jumbo* that appeared in America: "It is an amazing tour de force, witheringly scornful, gigantically clever, and at times devastatingly funny. . . . Apparently the underlying purpose of the satire is to drive home the lesson of simple faith. . . . The reader is assured of a mighty good time while he reads it."

CHAPTER SEVEN

A Life Dedicated to Art

❧

BACK AT LA NAPOULE, Henry Clews returned to his rocking chair in his studio, his sculptured figures grouped around him. The light was good, and Gonzales was there to prepare the armature of statues and busts and to make plaster casts. Henry put *Mumbo-Jumbo* out of his mind. He had not made one penny out of the whole affair. Grant Richards had declared himself bankrupt; nothing came in from America. So "Operation Mumbo-Jumbo" resolved itself into a few volumes on his bookshelf and memories. He again dedicated himself to sculpture.

Henry continued to create sculptural portraits and made of each bust a revelation of the sitter's character. The desire to understand the human soul and plumb its depths remained one of Clews's chief objectives all his life. As the technique of his art progressed, his works took on a soul-penetrating, clairvoyant aspect, full of psychological insight and seasoned with humor and irony. An idealist, Clews was often bitterly disappointed to find so little greatness in humanity. He only smiled at little human sins, for he knew he was an offender himself. It was the lack of great purpose or dedication to noble causes and high ideals that he deplored. He tried to challenge himself to such ideals in the creation of his art, and often said, "It does not much matter what you love, but you must love something with all your heart and soul. Then you become a living personality."

In the center of the courtyard at La Napoule, Clews set up The God of Humormystics, a figure of an old man atop a high column with a diverse group of characters around its base. Perhaps this work best exemplifies the values that Henry subscribed to as an artist and a man. The old god, a kindly, smiling figure, serenely holds out to all visitors the mystic rose of the spirit, a symbol of earthly and divine love. He tramples under his left foot a toad representing evil, and he releases from under his half-

Henry Clews in June 1934 before shrine at La Napoule. Marie's caption reads: "Sculptured boats show up well. They are in honor of Father's being a Naval Officer. Observe the Ms on the shrine. Architecture by me. Each stone measured and cut by me in cardboard. Sculptures by Henry."

raised right foot the head of a smiling woman, as if to say, "Arise, Woman, and work with me, be my inspiration." Around the base, a wreath of grotesque heads symbolizing vices are tempered by the presence of the heads of two innocent babes, the head of Mary the divine mother, and that of Mary Magdalene, the forgiven sinner. Near them, the dovelike Holy Spirit illuminates humanity. This garland of faces is held in place by a great serpent swallowing his tail, the symbol of eternity. Gathered around the base are Adam and Eve as children and Human Love. Little Love, pensive and introspective, also crushes with one foot an evil toad.

Clews exhibited this large statue in the galleries of Jacques Seligman and Company in New York in 1916. The press was strangely silent about it. It was, very simply, boycotted. A number of Henry's friends protested this treatment. Grant La Farge, the well-known architect, wrote to Henry to offer his support, enclosing a complaint he had written to *The New Republic* to chastise the critics for irresponsibly ignoring a significant work of art. But, most important, Frederick MacMonnies, an American sculptor whose works were much admired by Clews, sent a letter to

Henry. It was ample reward for Henry's artistic effort and consolation for his shabby treatment by the critics. He considered it his first serious recognition as a sculptor by a brother artist and carried this letter around with him for days:

22 East 62nd Street
New York
March 4th 1916

Dear Mr. Clews.

I went to see your statue the other day and was delighted with it.

It is a fine work, and a notable contribution to American art, and one of the most interesting pieces of modern sculpture.

You have "hitched your chariot to a star"… that is, sound design, without which sculpture is a poor affair… merely a transitory manifestation of the imitative instinct.

With your gifts, guided as you are by tradition and inspiring yourself directly from Nature, you have a straight road before you and a limitless horizon, and I wish you uninterrupted good health… you have everything else necessary to your happiness.

With gentle compliments to your wife, believe me,

Sincerely yours,
Frederick MacMonnies

And here is Clews's answer:

The Plaza
Fifth Avenue
Central Park
New York
March 6th 1916

Mon cher Maître:

Your letter touched me to the quick and I want to thank you with heart and mind for having written it.

It has come to me at the most critical moment of my career, and it is my first cornerstone of recognition.

You have filled our fireside with great happiness, and with your note under my pillow, we have dreamed of the future. What more can America offer me than the praise of her most distinguished artist?

Your letter is one of the greatest events of my life, and again I thank you for it with all my might and main.

Please present my compliments to your wife, and believe me

Very sincerely yours,
Henry Clews

Henry (center) and assistants hoist his "God of Humormystics" onto its pedestal in the courtyard at La Napoule, 1921

Henry and Marie at La Napoule in a 1928 photo by their son Mancha

THE GOD OF HUMORMYSTICS no doubt kept on smiling during his unnoticed visit to the Seligman Gallery, but surely he felt more at home in the courtyard of his creator at Château de La Napoule. He is the center, the heart of the château. All guests are greeted by him, all receive his blessings and his welcome as they enter this citadel of peace, art, and goodwill. The old fellow is proud that he was Henry's wedding present to Marie. Its plaque of rose marble is inscribed:

The God of Humormystics

Mancha — Marie

Dec. 19, 1914.

At La Napoule, there was a new challenge to face: the marriage of architecture and sculpture, which Henry, not having passed through art school, had to discover for himself. It was a long and painful process, but Clews preferred to be the master of his own world and to learn by observation and trial. To transform the château into a place more suitable as a dwelling, he developed abilities as a decorator.

MARIE HAD STUDIED in various art schools for a season or two and was able to draw with ease and a certain competence. Henry made her the architect, and she was able, with a little practice and study, to draw to scale all the plans for the château and to direct the master-mason, Cossano, and his son and brother in the building of the château. Many books of her drawings still exist.

Eventually the reconstruction and decoration of the château became the chief life and art interest of Marie and Henry. For many happy, prosperous, and creative years, they carried their ideas to completion.

Activity teemed around the courtyard between the old Saracen towers. A dozen stonecutters were engaged. They set up their workshop under a shed, to shelter themselves from rain and sun. Stones were piled all about. The château and the courtyard became a great studio workshop, which horrified the family, friends, and occasional visitors from America, who had expected to find the Clews family surrounded by green lawns, marble fountains, butlers, and cordon-bleu chefs.

When visitors drove through the great pentagonic stone gateposts (which were later taken down to make room for the present conciergerie, with its Renaissance pointed stone archway, sculptured by Clews) and up the driveway, flanked by a double row of eucalyptus trees, they were still hopeful that elegance would follow. But when they reached the courtyard filled with workmen's barracks, heaps of stones, and stonecutters naked to the waist, working hard; when they heard the chorus of chisels clicking on the stones and found Marie Clews in a painting apron supervising the stonecutters and giving out cardboard models for stones to be cut, they were dismayed.

"Why, the Clewses live like peasants, like workmen. Who would have thought of such a thing? Elsie (such people refused to call her Marie) used to be one of the most perfectly dressed women in America and Henry's mother the most exquisite perfectionist. How can she and Lucy Clews's son live like common working people?"

They sometimes complained to Henry and Marie. "The house is all right, once you get into it," they said, "clean and even pretty; you have a good cook and a nice little motor, but why, why should the courtyard look like a dump heap, and why must all those dirty, naked men be chipping stone right under your noses?"

"My dear American friends," Henry would say, "I deeply appreciate your very flattering solicitude concerning the state of my soul . . . my courtyard, I mean. One day, I suppose, that courtyard will be clean and tidy, but I will no longer be there to see it. For when work stops, life stops, creation stops. Creation is born from disorder and generates order. I sympathize with your fears, dear Mr. Jones, for there is indeed a dangerous creative spirit loose in La Napoule. Let us drown these fears in spirits . . . I mean, let us go and have a drink, and we will all feel better."

"Better leave that cranky Clews and his wife alone," said Mr. Jones to Mrs. Jones and the Misses Jones on their way back to Cannes.

"Rather a pity," said Mrs. Jones with disgust. "I had thought of asking Elsie to tea next week to meet the duchess of X, but of course, I won't now."

It is true that the courtyard of Château de La Napoule was very untidy, but out of those ungainly heaps of stones emerged a whole cloister, Romanesque Gothic in feeling, with columns of rose, gray, and jade green porphyry from the nearby Esterel quarries. Each column was topped by a capital sculptured by Clews. Their subjects are imaginary creatures, part human, part beast.

Henry and Marie continued to work on La Napoule from 1919 until 1937, when Henry died. It has now become again, as it was some centuries ago, an interesting historical château, a landmark of the Mediterranean coast, unique in its picturesqueness, in the romance and wild beauty of its situation. It is both a memorial to the talent of Henry Clews Jr. and a celebration of American art and culture. Marie has done everything she can to follow Henry's wishes and preserve La Napoule for the enjoyment and inspiration of future generations.

MYSTICS AND PSYCHICS tell us that among people there are new spirits and old spirits. Some have never lived before and are starting out on the long path of reincarnation. But the old ones have passed through many bodily forms and carry, in their subconscious, ancient memories and remarkable knowledge of life.

Upon entering a city new to them or a house they have previously never visited, such persons may have the sensation that they have been there before. They seem haunted by the certainty that during some former existence they have spent part of their lives in such a place. The old soul also recognizes people he has known before. He feels sure that his present life is only a further chapter of the great book of his spiritual evolution.

Such deep intuition and uncanny wisdom are sometimes called

genius. From such heightened perception and unconscious knowledge springs all that is fine, original, inspiring. The great inventors, statesmen, scientists, and artists all carry within them that spark of inspiration, an offshoot of the divine. Not all old souls attain to greatness in their fields, but all are apt to become "life givers" within the circles where their lives are passed, for they transmit that spark to their friends and neighbors.

Henry surely was an old soul, and the evidence of this lies in the legacy of art he left at La Napoule.

As MARIE MOVES ABOUT the house or wanders in the gardens, she is always conscious of Henry's love, conscious that she must carry on her work of hospitality and the creation of beauty, until she, too, takes her last rest by Henry's side, in the tomb she lovingly fashioned for him when he "laid himself down to sleep."

At the portals of the Golden Gates, the recording angel may one day say, "Marie, formerly Elsie."

Henry as he died in 1937, surrounded by birds. The photo is by his son Mancha.

The cloister at La Napoule

The former Elsie will answer, "My name is Marie, and by that name and no other do I wish to be judged, for it was given me by Henry, arbiter of my new life and my new world. My fate and my destiny, our destiny, Henry's and mine, is oriented toward Marie. Let it be Henry and Marie, and let all the stones speak for us—the intertwined H and M encircled by two Cs—on every lintel, every mantel, every capital and column of La Napoule. Here Henry and Marie lived out their lives, here Henry laid himself down for his long sleep, and here Marie will join him one day.

Every hundred years they will speak through the silence of the tomb: "Are you there, Marie?"

And the answer will come: "I am here, Henry, close beside you."

And then silence will envelop them again for another hundred years, except for the lapping of the waves of the blue Mediterranean, the hoot of the little owls, and the trill of the larks and the nightingales swinging in the tall straight cypress trees that stand as guardians to the Tower of La Mancha, where two lovers are resting awhile, side by side, never to be separated again.

Afterword
MARGARET STRAWBRIDGE CLEWS

❧

IN HER MEMOIRS, MARIE CLEWS does not dwell on life at La Napoule after her husband's death, though she did in fact live there for twenty-two more years. A lot happened in that time that I wish to record.

Immediately after Henry's death, Marie set about preparing his tomb at La Napoule and supervised the ongoing building projects there. She also made arrangements for Henry Clews's sculpture to be exhibited at the Metropolitan Museum of Art in New York City early in 1939. It was the first display of his work in the United States since 1914.

When war broke out in 1939, Marie did not leave France, as most American expatriates did. She knew that if she returned to the United States, even to visit for a short while, her passport would be revoked for the duration of the war. Instead, with Miss Coles to assist her, she chose to stay at La Napoule to defend the château and the treasured sculptures her husband had created. This courageous move was typical of her strength of will. From the time France fell to Germany in 1940 up to the landing of the Allied Army of Liberation along the Riviera in August 1944, she held her course.

After the fall of France, the French Riviera near the Italian border was first occupied by the Italians and then by the Germans. Marie had managed to have some of her husband's sculptures hidden away in a small chapel in the hills for safekeeping. She also had the carved capitals removed from the columns of the cloister and replaced by blocks of wood; then the capitals were buried on the grounds to protect them. The sculpture that now dominates the courtyard, the God of Humormystics, was also buried.

Because of the important position of La Napoule on the coastline, the Germans built gun emplacements in the courtyard and kept an eye on the château. They even broke into Henry Clews's tomb to see if ammunition had been hidden there. At one point, Marie was pressed into offering hospitality to the officers. She managed to scrounge up a chicken and some wine, and these were served to the Germans. When they asked for a place to sleep, she showed them that all the furniture had been removed from the bedrooms (she had also stored them away, along with the doors Henry had carved), and so the Germans stayed elsewhere. She managed to resist their attempts to put her out of the château until, shortly before the Allies broke through, the German soldiers finally insisted that she leave. She stayed for a short time in a friend's house about a mile away.

The first beachhead that the Allies gained on the Mediterranean coast in 1944 included La Napoule. After the war, Marie noted to a reporter from the *Philadelphia Evening Bulletin,* "The most wonderful sight of my life was the American flag flying from the battleships circling in the cove below. Gliders laden with troops from Africa passed right over my head . . . and I could see colored parachutes drifting down like showers of flowers."

On one of those first happy days, she saw, running toward her on the beach, a disheveled young man with a beard and dressed in army fatigues; he gave her a big bearhug and cried, "Hello, Cousin Marie!" It was her cousin Sarah Whelen's son-in-law from Philadelphia, Lew Van Dusen. What a joy for them to meet this way as that terrible war was ending!

Though a great relief to the French people in general, the arrival of the Allied Forces brought danger for Marie. Her gardener, whom she had fired for incompetence, denounced her to the Allied authorities as a collaborator with the Germans—a serious charge. (The gardener later became the leader of the Communists in Cannes.) True, she had given the Germans hospitality, but what else could she have done? It would have been impossible for her and for Miss Coles, two single women, to deny the invading Germans access to the chateau. It certainly did not mean that Marie had welcomed the German occupation of France!

She was helped out of this tough spot by a navy lieutenant who had arrived with the Army of Liberation—Dick Henry, a family friend. Without getting permission from his commanding officer, he wrote two notes, one in French and one in English, which he gave to Marie. They stated that Mrs. Henry Clews was under the protection of the U.S. Navy. When the authorities arrived to take her to jail, producing these notes saved her from harassment and possibly a worse fate—some of those accused of collaboration were executed.

৵৻

LA NAPOULE WAS NOT MUCH DAMAGED by the war. Some shells had hit the roof, but it wasn't too difficult to patch it up. When Marie wondered what to do about the big concrete gun emplacements in the courtyard, I suggested that she simply grow ivy over them. They look very nice that way. The gardener still uses them to store his wheelbarrow and rakes.

Concerning her refusal to leave France, the *Evening Bulletin* quotes Marie as saying, "I'm glad I did; my neighbors who fled lost everything." About the communist gardener's accusation, she stated, "That was a common trick . . . the gardeners . . . took possession of villas after the owners had been sent away, sold the furniture, and blamed it on the occupation troops." Because of Marie's pluck and determination, La Napoule had survived the war, and, most important to her, none of her husband's sculptures had been lost or damaged.

After enduring her husband's long illness and the war that followed shortly after his death, Marie was ready to put these trying times behind her and "kick up her heels" a bit. She bought a small house in New York City overlooking Gramercy Park, between the Belgian embassy and the home of the actors Alfred Lunt and Lynn Fontaine. She often stayed there during the winter, enjoying the opera and theater and visiting friends and family, while Miss Coles managed the château at La Napoule.

She socialized a good deal more than was possible during her husband's life; he had preferred a quiet, cloistered existence. She offered hospitality to some members of the European aristocracy who had fallen on hard times, and they often stayed with her for a bit. One of them, the Archduke Otto von Hapsburg, was so impoverished that his sister had to sew for her living at a couturiére in Paris. Marie also put on some wonderful entertainments; for example, the pianist Van Cliburn performed at La Napoule at a private party.

Marie made sure that her husband's works continued to be shown to the public. In the 1940s and 1950s, exhibitions were arranged in Philadelphia, Nice, and Paris. (A small exhibit arranged by Mancha and

Marie with her twin grandsons, Kit and Henry Clews, 1946

me at The Cosmopolitan Club in Philadelphia was very well received by the members, many of whom are themselves artists and professional women.) Marie also continued to pour her energy into improving the château. She planned a new wing to provide gallery space. She was also considering the long-term future of La Napoule—how could she best preserve the legacy of her husband's sculpture and its imaginative, fairy-tale setting? What purposes should it serve in the decades ahead?

※

I MET MARIE CLEWS after the war. I had married her son Mancha in 1940, but the war had prevented her from coming to our wedding, and it kept us from visiting her. We sent her Care packages of tea and chocolate and tried to stay in touch. At the end of the war, she traveled to New York where she stayed with a cousin; then she came to visit us in Pennsylvania.

I was fascinated by Marie Clews. She was almost six feet tall and stunningly beautiful. She spoke with me quite frankly about her marriage, which, in contrast to her description in her memoirs, had been terribly difficult. Henry Clews was susceptible to depression (a term that wasn't mentioned in public in those days), and she was always concerned about his well-being. She made sure that either she or Miss Coles was ever on hand to watch over him. The secluded life they led was often lonely for her, and she kept up subscriptions to American magazines and had a clipping service send her newspaper columns about society happenings in her old haunts. She had been ostracized by those who thought her marriage to Henry Clews would be a mistake. But all her life she truly believed in his talent, and I don't think she regretted spending her life with him.

I admired Marie for many things: her courage in remaining at La Napoule during the war years, her tremendous drive to make art the center of their life together, and her gift of conveying enthusiasm for her project to those around her.

My husband Mancha and I first visited La Napoule together in 1948. We stayed in Mancha's old bedroom with its remarkably narrow bed, which we happily shared! Marie took us to a tea party with the Duke and Duchess of Windsor, which was exciting. The Duke reminisced about my father's uncle Bob, with whom he had fox-hunted both in England and in the United States. The Duchess was dressed quite simply in white, and she wore her emeralds; she was very gracious to us.

At another time in the south of France, Marie took us to tea with the society columnist Elsa Maxwell. I remember that Elsa admired my hairstyle of thick, twisted braids which Mancha had designed for me. In Paris, Marie gave a luncheon for Otto von Hapsburg, the nephew of the Hapsburg heir. Marie expected me to curtsy to him, but, being an independent Quaker, I resisted. (Quakers have historically refused to bow to anyone, since we believe that every person is equal in God's sight.) She was a bit disappointed in me, but we smoothed over our differences eventually.

※

SINCE THE TIME of her husband's death, Marie had been dreaming of plans for establishing La Napoule as a permanent memorial to her husband and his work. In our conversations, I spoke with her about how I, as a young girl, had dreamed of studying art in Europe. (I had studied at the Pennsylvania Academy of the Fine Arts in Philadelphia.) Though this desire never materialized for me, I suggested to her how wonderful it would be for other students to have such an opportunity. The idea seemed to grow on her, although, as she said at first, she wasn't sure she wanted to have long-haired art students dropping cigarette ashes on her husband's sculpture! But I think she meant this in jest.

Then she decided she would really like to help give a talented young person a start. A friend of mine from Philadelphia—the sculptor Edward Fenno Hoffman—became the first artist-in-residence at La Napoule. He had won the Prix de Rome, but, because he did not wish to be parted from his wife and young child (a condition of the prize), he did not accept it. So Marie invited him, together with his family, to stay at La Napoule so that he could singlemindedly pursue his creative work. Though they initially planned to stay for two months, the time actually stretched to two years! It was a most productive experience for Hoffman, who completed forty works of sculpture there. Marie later invited other artists to live and work there.

During one of Marie's visits to us, she consulted a lawyer in Philadelphia about setting up La Napoule as a charitable foundation—a memorial to Henry Clews and a celebration of American art and culture. The Philadelphia lawyer advised her against it, recommending that she simply leave the château to her children and let them decide what to do with it.

*Marie Clews (right) and Miss Coles (left) with
Diane and Ogden Goelet after their civil
marriage, October 8, 1955.*

Later, she met a more sympathetic lawyer, David Colton, who became an enthusiastic supporter of Marie's hopes and plans for La Napoule. He worked hard, for little cost, to find the best avenue to achieve this. Through his efforts, in 1950, the State University of New York granted an absolute charter to the trustees of La Napoule, and the government of France formally recognized it as an American institution in their country. In the charter David Colton included the following explanation of La Napoule Art Foundation:

> Among its purposes are to exhibit and publicize the works of art of Henry Clews and the works of art of other sculptors, artists and others engaged in any of the fine arts; and "to promote in France and in other countries having a keen interest in the fine arts a greater appreciation of the work of citizens of the United Sates of America."

> We, the Trustees, are grateful to the Government of France and its Ministers, who have accorded our Foundation the recognition of educational status to operate as a foreign association in La Napoule, and for the fine spirit of cooperation of the governmental and local officials of the Alpes Maritimes.

Trustees of La Napoule meeting in 1994. Back row: William P. Wood, Christopher S. Clews, Noele M. Clews, Henry M. Clews; middle row: Margaret Strawbridge Clews, Mary Judge; front row: Mary Holland, Brigitte Clews Crompton, The Duke of Argyll.

According to the stipulations of this agreement, La Napoule Art Foundation was to maintain and manage the property for purposes of education and cultural enrichment. Marie was the first president of the foundation. The first trustees of the foundation were Marie Elsie Clews, Ethelberte M. Coles, Mary Ann Robertson, Leta Clews Cromwell, Mancha Madison Clews, Evan Potter, and David Colton. Until her death in 1959, Marie was much occupied in setting up the specific terms of the trust. Again, David Colton gave legal assistance and guidance; Mancha handled the French paperwork, since he is fluent in the language. Marie was able to sign the final documents shortly before her death, and her initial endowment helped set the foundation on a sound financial footing.

Marie died knowing that her life's work had been accomplished. She had nurtured the talents of the artist Henry Clews, Jr., helped create a remarkable villa, and left a legacy of beauty and inspiration for those who would enjoy La Napoule in the future.

৵৻

I N A S E N S E, L A N A P O U L E continues as a work in progress. New programs, such as seminars in landscape design, have been created, and artists from around the world stay at La Napoule to work on their creative projects in an inspiring setting. Their presence lends a vitality to La Napoule that makes it more than a typical museum; while celebrating works of art of the past, it also nurtures artists, writers, and musicians of the future. Also, during the summer, the public is invited to tour the buildings and grounds, and space can be rented for conferences, meetings, weddings, and other celebrations.

Marie Clews would be especially proud, I think, of her family's continued interest and support of the foundation. Her grandson, Christopher (Kit) Clews is president; her grandson Henry is a member of the board of trustees, as are Brigitte Clews Crompton, her husband's granddaughter, and Ian Argyll, her husband's grandson. I, her daughter-in-law, am also a board member, and lastly there is her Philadelphia lawyer cousin Lewis H. Van Dusen, whose son, Lewis H. Van Dusen III wrote an excellent senior thesis in art and archeology at Princeton University in 1962) on Henry Clews, Jr., entitled "The Life and Works of the Sculptor". This treatise so enthusiastically undertaken by her young cousin promoted a renewed interest in Henry Clews. In 1983 Marie's grandson Kit Clews, who had graduated from the University of Pennsylvania with a master's degree in architecture, organized with his wife Noele (a landscape designer) a sort of "Tom Sawyer" work group to go there; together these young people paid, in effect, to paint and to repair some of the buildings at La Napoule. This was the beginning of the Château's rejuvenation.

Thus, Marie's "impossible dream" began to be realized.

A final note: As this book was going to press, we learned that Stephanie Crompton, Henry Clews's great-granddaughter, recently had written her graduating thesis in art history at St. Andrews University in Scotland on "The Art of Henry Clews," a fact that would, I think, give Marie great satisfaction.

Margaret and Mancha Clews flanked by sons Henry and Kit at La Napoule.

WE WISH TO THANK our neighbors in Kendal at Hanover for encouraging us to edit and publish Marie Clews's story: Betty and Boyce Price, their friend Professor Joe Medlicott, and Suzanne Levi. We are deeply grateful for the patient and constant support of our sons, Henry and Kit Clews. Finally we wish to thank Henry McIlvaine Parsons and his Grace, the Duke of Argyll, for their kind words of endorsement; our faithful friend Helen B. Zimmerman for her literary acumen; and the gifted people of Memoirs Unlimited, Webster Bull and Susanna Brougham, who made our book possible through their talented editing and designing.

Margaret Strawbridge Clews
Mancha Madison Clews